CHAUCER'S POETICS
AND THE MODERN READER

CHAUCER'S POETICS AND THE MODERN READER

ROBERT M. JORDAN

University of California Press
Berkeley   Los Angeles   London

University of California Press
Berkeley and Los Angeles, California

University of California Press, Ltd.
London, England

© 1987 by
The Regents of the University of California

Library of Congress Cataloging-in-Publication Data
Jordan, Robert M.
   Chaucer's poetics and the modern reader.
   Includes index.
   1. Chaucer's Geoffrey, d. 1400—Technique.
2. Rhetoric, Medieval.   3. Poetics.   4. Reader-response
criticism.   I. Title.
PR1940.J67   1987   821'.1   86-24920
ISBN 0-520-05977-8 (alk. paper)

Printed in the United States of America

1   2   3   4   5   6   7   8   9

To the memory of my son
John Sebert Jordan
1952–1979

Contents

Acknowledgments

I am grateful to the University of British Columbia for the year's study leave that enabled me to complete this book. For fellowship support, it is a pleasure to express my thanks to the Social Sciences and Humanities Research Council of Canada and to the Izaak Walton Killam Foundation, two institutions that have contributed significantly to the advancement of research in the humanities in Canada.

My quotations from Chaucer are taken from F. N. Robinson's edition of the *Complete Works* (1957), whose publisher, Houghton Mifflin Co., has kindly granted permission. I thank the editors of the *Chaucer Review* for permission to reprint, in substantially revised form, studies of the *Book of the Duchess* and the *House of Fame* that originally appeared as articles in that journal. My chapter on the *Parlement of Foules* originally appeared in shorter form in *English Studies in Canada*, whose editors I thank for permission to reprint.

My colleagues Andrew Busza, Lee Johnson, and Grosvenor Powell contributed moral, intellectual, and technical support during the gestation of this book, and Doreen Todhunter cheerfully conducted the manuscript through word processing and the early stages of editing. At the University of California Press Stephanie Fay's sensitive copyediting saved me from numerous infelicities of expression. At home I was sustained through many difficult times by the encouragement and understanding of my wife, Jean, whose devotion has made all the difference.

Introduction

It is now widely acknowledged that realist interpretation does not fully account for the complexity of Chaucerian narrative. As a criterion of literary value "truth to life" is no longer satisfactory, for it begs the questions that seem critical today—whose truth and whose life, seen from what perspective and expressed in what form? These are questions about the validity of universals, of fixed, immutable truths, and they were as prominent and controversial in Chaucer's time as they are today. When old coherences dissolve under the challenge of logical and empirical analysis, seekers after truth—be they philosophers, scientists, or poets—find their subject of inquiry to be not the universe, God, and the soul, or even the good and the bad or the right and the wrong, but rather the language used by those who talk about such matters. Historians of philosophy have observed a parallel between the *via moderna* of fourteenth-century nominalism and the turn to analytical and positivist philosophy in the twentieth century, both movements disavowing a unified, universally acknowledged reality—the Augustinian synthesis in the fourteenth century and the Copernican and Newtonian world-frame in the twentieth—and turning instead to the language system as the object of logical and critical analysis. The program of the fourteenth-century nominalists ignited as much controversy as that of the twentieth-century positivists, and both movements register an increasing cultural uncertainty about fundamental values, including, of course, literary values.

Chaucer's poetry exhibits many forms of ambivalence about "truth" and considerable self-consciousness and anxiety about its own validity as an instrument of truth. While seemingly confident, often even flamboyant, in its command of the verbal medium, Chaucer's poetry also expresses, as I hope to make clear, a fragmented and problematic outlook, an uncertainty about fundamental truths, including the truth of poetry—indeed of language—and about the role and status of the poet. My purpose in this study is to derive from an analysis of Chaucer's poetry a poetics, a theory sufficiently consistent to account for a body of poetry whose coherences and meanings appear to be contingent and ambiguous rather than confidently authoritative and whose aesthetic values appear to be disjunctive and "inorganic" rather than consistent and "unified." Readers of a realist persuasion are likely to regard such a poetics as destructive of the verities of character and meaning, but I hope to demonstrate to the contrary that a poetics based on ambivalence and uncertainty nevertheless possesses aesthetic integrity and speaks to a human condition we can recognize as our own.

While my *Chaucer and the Shape of Creation* located some of the prefigurations of a Chaucerian poetics in the principles and practices of medieval architectonics, the present study is concerned with language theory. It approaches Chaucer from the other end of history, so to speak, taking advantage of the notable advances in the fields of linguistics and critical theory that have occurred since the publication of my earlier book. Some Chaucerians may regard such an approach as unmedieval and therefore irrelevant, but I think analysis of the textual evidence will demonstrate both the relevance and the validity of modern theory.

My opening chapter draws on the critical theory and authorial practices of our own time—works of "postmodern" theory and so-called avant-garde or "experimental" writing—to clarify the idea of a rhetorical poetics and to establish the grounds for claiming a close relation between postmodern and Chaucerian presuppositions about the nature of language and its role and efficacy in creating literary fictions. In contrast I cite the examples of Dickens and Henry James to illustrate how a realist poetics posits a fundamentally different assessment of the relation between language and reality. The result, I think, is not a distorted modernization of Chaucer

but a fuller realization of his place in a tradition of great literary artificers, a tradition that he founded in English but that
goes back to classical antiquity and forward to our own time.
The current rehabilitation of rhetoric as an intellectual disci-
pline has helped to reestablish literary values that were alien
to earlier generations of Chaucerians but were the bedrock
that underlay Chaucer's idea of poetry. Rhetoric is a slippery
foundation for an enduring monument to truth, and the ice
mountain in the *House of Fame* is a fitting sign of Chaucer's
awareness of the problematic nature of his medium.

Chapter 2 begins my study of Chaucer's works with the
House of Fame because that poem provides the clearest evidence—both in its scattered authorial comments and in its
disjunct structure and its flamboyant, self-reflexive style—of
the unspoken aesthetic and philosophical principles that
govern Chaucer's entire career. This "experimental" work displays Chaucer's delight in verbal artifice as well as his doubts
about the possibility of arriving at authoritative meaning
through the otherwise wonderful medium of language. Brilliantly displaying this authorial ambivalence, the *House of
Fame* at the same time adumbrates the semantic, structural,
and epistemological principles of a rhetorical poetics.

Following my discussion of the *House of Fame* I devote a
chapter to each of the other dream visions, viewing them as
variations on the poetics adduced in the *House of Fame*. The
discussion of the *Canterbury Tales* that follows in the closing
chapters is not intended to demonstrate a chronological development in Chaucer's career, from rhetor to realist, as an earlier
view maintained. Rather I wish to demonstrate the consistency
of Chaucer's aesthetic principles and philosophical outlook. I
wish also to illustrate the scope of his rhetorical poetics and
its adaptability to different kinds of subject matter.

Chapters 6 and 7 examine the beginning and the ending of
the *Canterbury Tales* and selected tales in between. The discussion of the General Prologue explores the relationship
between the Canterbury frame and the theoretical model
educed from the dream visions. I then single out two tales to
suggest the literary and aesthetic diversity attainable within

Chaucer's poetics of verbal artifice, the Pardoner's for its qualified realism and the Nun's Priest's for its unabashed rhetorical
virtuosity.

Chapter 7 examines the sequence that closes the *Canterbury
Tales*—the last fiction that is the Manciple's Tale, the last discourse that is the Parson's Tale, and the Retraction. In this sequence Chaucer once again attempts to resolve the ambivalence expressed in the *House of Fame* about the nature and
validity of the writer's labors. The paradoxical implications of
Chaucer's rejection of the ambiguities of poetics in favor of the
certitude of theology are the subject of my concluding pages.

1

Poetics and Rhetoric

Despite resistance from many quarters—such as the old philology and the New Criticism—studies in literary theory, or poetics, have proliferated in recent years and are producing significant changes in the nature and direction of literary studies. New questions are being asked of old texts, questions that are more analytical than interpretive and are directed not toward naming the meaning of a particular work but toward gaining a knowledge of the general laws that preside over its status as a work of literary discourse. After a period of vital activity, conducted largely under the aegis of the New Criticism, interpretive studies appear to be reaching the point of exhaustion. In Chaucer studies as elsewhere we have seen interpretations of particular works, carried out with insight and ingenuity, produce contradictory but often equally persuasive results. It is becoming increasingly difficult to deny the ennui that threatens to envelop Chaucer studies at the appearance of every new reading of *Troilus* or every new version of the Pardoner's condition.

In his *Introduction to Poetics* Tzvetan Todorov proposes to redress what he observes to be the "massive imbalance in favor of interpretation [that] characterizes the history of literary studies."[1] He contrasts poetics, or literary analysis, with interpretation, noting that interpretation, in seeking to make the text speak, places its fidelity in the *other* that is external to literature. It seeks to capture the referents of literary discourse, be they as concrete as characters and settings or as abstract as

1. Tzvetan Todorov, *Introduction to Poetics*, trans. Richard Howard, Theory and History of Literature, vol. 1 (Minneapolis: Univ. of Minnesota Press, 1981), p. 7.

moral or spiritual messages. Poetics, in contrast, aims at principles of literariness. It seeks objective description that is empirically verifiable and independent of the historical and psychological contingencies of interpretive readings. In a comprehensive theory of literature, analysis and interpretation are reciprocal tendencies, equally valid. Both start with the text, but their goals are distinct from each other. The aim of modern poetics is to explore a field of inquiry that lies outside the scope of most interpretive studies.

The present study of Chaucer's works employs methods of literary analysis in an effort to redress for Chaucer studies some of the imbalance Todorov speaks of. It seeks to discover the general principles that shaped Chaucer's understanding of the nature and significance of poetry. Although Chaucer formulated no systematic theory of poetry, we know that this question was important to him. He discusses it explicitly in several contexts—most notably, perhaps, in the *House of Fame*. And he explores it indirectly as well, through irony and parodic play in a variety of contexts throughout his works, from the *Book of the Duchess* to the Parson's Prologue and the Retraction. It underlies the self-conscious posturings of the *Troilus* narrator, for example, as in his overtly expressed concern about fidelity to his "source," his ambivalence about his audience—hearers or readers, pagan or Christian?—his anxiety about the correctness of his language and about the meaning of what he has written. These and innumerable other forms of attentiveness to the labor of writing are the traces of Chaucer's poetics, his idea of poetry. These open displays of artistic self-consciousness, highlighting the author's relationship to his verbal medium, denote an idea of poetry that is best characterized as rhetorical. In speaking of Chaucer's poetics as rhetorical I am elaborating a linkage that Robert Payne firmly established two decades ago, based on the medieval understanding of rhetoric as concerned with written composition rather than public oratory.[2] The term *rhetorical* applies both in

2. Robert O. Payne, *The Key of Remembrance: A Study of Chaucer's Poetics* (New Haven, Conn.: Yale Univ. Press, 1963), pp. 9–59. The antique understanding of rhetoric as persuasive oral discourse did not survive the Christian

the narrower sense of poetry as blocks of language crafted and ordered by the poet and in the broader philosophical sense of a relationship between language and truth that is problematic and that questions the nature—and even the possibility—of meaning. Primary emphasis on language—its tangible, material nature and its uncertain relation to truth—distinguishes rhetorical poetics from the poetics of realism. The implications of this distinction will concern us throughout this study.

If in the popular mind rhetoric still bears something of the stigma of dishonest persuasion, a vestige of the nineteenth century's aversion to visible artifice and its bias in favor of "natural" expression,[3] rhetoric is faring better in the academic mind. Wayne Booth's *Rhetoric of Fiction* effectively demonstrated the practical impossibility of an author's choosing to avoid rhetoric: "He can choose only the kind of rhetoric he will employ."[4] Richard Lanham accounts for the puzzling history of rhetoric—why it has been so deplored and why it has so endured—by finding that the rhetorical self is one half of the "complex, creative, unstable, painful" consciousness of Western man. The opening chapter of his *Motives of Eloquence* is a philosophical defense of *homo rhetoricus* as an equal and contending partner to *homo seriosus* in the history of Western

---

Middle Ages except insofar as the *artes praedicandi* of the twelfth and thirteenth centuries adapted it to the constraints of Christian pulpit oratory. For the most part the so-called rhetorical handbooks, such as Geoffrey of Vinsauf's *Poetria nova*, to which Chaucer alludes in *Troilus* and the Nun's Priest's Tale, dealt with language in written form. This "apparatus of rhetorical techniques clustering around discourse or art forms" is what George Kennedy describes as "secondary rhetoric," a "slippage" from persuasion to narration, from civic to personal contexts, and from oral discourse to literature, including poetry (*Classical Rhetoric and Its Christian and Secular Tradition from Ancient to Modern Times* [Chapel Hill: Univ. of North Carolina Press, 1980], p. 5). The definitive history of medieval rhetoric is James J. Murphy, *Rhetoric in the Middle Ages: A History of Rhetorical Theory from St. Augustine to the Renaissance* (Berkeley: Univ. of California Press, 1974).

3. See, for example, Ruskin's definition of rhetoric as a base study, suitable "exclusively for men who desire to deceive or be deceived" (*Stones of Venice* [London: Dent, n.d.], vol. 3, p. 97).

4. Wayne C. Booth, *The Rhetoric of Fiction* (Chicago: Univ. of Chicago Press, 1961), p. 49.

man.[5] Rhetorical man centers his vital awareness on the word. He develops an overpowering self-consciousness about language. His orientation to life is social and pragmatic, committed to no single construction of the world, no single set of values. Unlike serious man, rhetorical man disavows concern for a central self and a unified reality, "and if he relinquishes the luxury of a central self, a soul, he gains the tolerance, and usually the sense of humor, that comes from knowing he— and others—not only may *think* differently, but may *be* differently" (p. 5).

The rhetorical cast of Chaucer's authorial vision is strikingly adumbrated in Lanham's synthesized portrait of a rhetorical education:

> Start your student young. Teach him a minute concentration on the word, how to write it, speak it, remember it. . . . Let words come first as objects and sounds long before they can, for a child, take on full meaning. They are looked *at* before they can be looked through. From the beginning, stress behavior as performance, reading aloud, speaking with gesture, a full range of histrionic adornment. Require no original thought. Demand instead an agile marshaling of the proverbial wisdom on any issue. Categorize this wisdom into predigested units, commonplaces, *topoi.* Dwell on their decorous fit into situation. Develop elaborate memory schemes to keep them readily at hand. Teach, as theory of personality, a corresponding set of accepted personality types, a taxonomy of impersonation. Drill the student incessantly on correspondences between verbal style and personality type, life style. Nourish an acute sense of social situation. Let him, to weariness, translate, not only from one language to another, but from one style to another.[6]

5. Richard A. Lanham, *The Motives of Eloquence: Literary Rhetoric in the Renaissance* (New Haven, Conn.: Yale Univ. Press, 1976). Stephen Manning explores the usefulness for Chaucer criticism of Lanham's *homo rhetoricus* as well as Johan Huizinga's *homo ludens* in a provocative essay, "Rhetoric, Game, Morality, and Geoffrey Chaucer," *Studies in the Age of Chaucer* 1 (1979): 105–18.

6. Lanham, p. 2. Lanham's program captures the spirit of the late medieval idea of a rhetorical education, as expounded by the handbooks of Geoffrey of Vinsauf and others, with its emphasis on language as a tangible medium to be manipulated and "moulded" by the trained rhetor. In this respect medieval teachers sustained the classical tradition, but notably absent

Perhaps the purest Chaucerian distillation of these principles is the Nun's Priest's Tale, which fairly crackles with "predigested units" of proverbial wisdom and with a multiplicity of viewpoints culled from diverse sources, all set against one another in a tour de force of stylistic play. But we find the same fascination with verbal surfaces, with words as quantities to be skillfully deployed, throughout Chaucer's works. The *Canterbury Tales* preeminently, but *Troilus* and the dream visions as well, display Chaucer's "taxonomy of impersonation," his cultivated consciousness of correspondences between verbal style and personality type. Not the least of Chaucer's manifest concerns is the verbal representation of his own personality. Plainly he did not aim to refine himself out of existence, but neither did he aim to represent himself unambiguously. The many guises he adopted in his varied impersonations of speakers who self-consciously intrude on their stories—including those designated or implied to be "Chaucer" as well as those speaking under other names—bespeak a complex view of fictional technique, a poetics more generous and comprehensive than the requirements of a realist poetics would allow.

The presuppositions that shaped the pioneer modern criticism of Chaucer were of a distinctly realist cast, grounded in the value criteria of verisimilitude and social realism. Rhetorical analysis, in contrast, educes underlying values of a distinctly "artificial" sort. Henry James's influential formulation of realist values serves as a useful negative touchstone in articulating the rhetorical values of Chaucerian narrative. In "The Art of Fiction" James defined the novel as "a living thing, all one and continuous," which eschewed artifice and the signs of authorship and cultivated a seamless fusion with the reality it addressed, a reality that James and his world confidently assumed to be there, one and continuous, perceptible to all who were sufficiently cultivated and sensitive to

---

from their teachings is the emphasis on the moral and intellectual standards required by the ideal orator-philosopher and good citizen of the *polis* in, for example, Quintilian's *Institutio oratoria*.

apprehend it.[7] When James declared, "I cannot imagine composition existing in a series of blocks," he was de-quantifying
the medium, rendering it invisible or at least porous, his aim
being to assure that language did not attract attention to itself
and thereby impede the flow of perception between reader
and reality. James's realist view of fiction as "an art that undertakes so immediately to reproduce life" depended on the assumptions that language is virtually transparent and that life
is univalent and accurately perceptible through it.

Evidence that Chaucer was a writer of a different persuasion
comes readily to hand. From those compositional artifices that
impart a distinctly non-Jamesian structural disjunctiveness
and stylistic flamboyance we can infer presuppositions that
Chaucer himself might have articulated if he had been a writer
of critical essays. To formulate such a poetics is the purpose of
the chapters that follow, but it may be anticipated here that
Chaucer was not as confident as Henry James about the relation of language to reality. His ambivalence reflects the outlook of rhetorical man, who cannot be univalent about anything, including particularly himself and his art, without
violating his own nature and rendering himself "serious."
Chaucer's works display an uneasiness with univalent authority, be it historical authority, moral authority, or the authority of language. His unspoken poetics provides a framework for coming to terms with uncertainty.

Rhetoric provides the basis for a poetics of uncertainty—or
to put it more positively, a pluralistic poetics—because of its
primary and always manifest presupposition that language is
conventional and inevitably ambiguous; it is a system devised
and managed by man, rather than a univocal emanation from
God and the created world. The crucial difference between
rhetoric and realism in this regard is dramatically illustrated
in the career of St. Augustine. When the teacher of pagan
rhetoric was converted to Christianity, he gave up words for

7. Henry James, "The Art of Fiction," in *Partial Portraits* (London: Macmillan, 1911), pp. 384, 391–92. Published as a lecture in 1884, this essay is
now widely anthologized.

the Word and became the most influential formulator and teacher of the orthodoxy usually designated by his name, the Augustinian synthesis. With the certainty of revealed truth at its core, Christian doctrine left little scope for doubt or for empirical investigation. Its method was not analysis but interpretation and reaffirmation of "the Word [that] was made flesh and dwelt among us." The Bible, God's Word, was the only valid text, and it linked man indissolubly with Truth. Christian allegoresis was a method of interpreting the world in accordance with God's univocal Truth.[8]

Historians of philosophy tell us that the dissolution of the Augustinian synthesis coincided with the fourteenth century's preoccupation with the divergent conditions of revealed truth and natural knowledge, a preoccupation that inaugurated the split between theology and philosophy and opened new avenues of inquiry. Gordon Leff has described the "overall loss of coherence" and the new pluralism initiated by the nominalist *via moderna:*

> There were not only new alignments but a new pluralism, which in its scientific aspects might almost be called a positivism. It is striking that greater advances were made in the fourteenth century in mathematics, physical theory, and logic than at any other time in the Middle Ages before or after. . . . Moreover, hardly less striking, they were to a great extent pursued independently of the theological and philosophical questions from which they had originated, having their own modes of expression and literary forms in the different kinds of treatises on proportions, calculations, and logical *sophismata.*[9]

8. For a study of the challenge fiction presented to the medieval understanding of the truth of God's "book" of creation, see Jesse Gellrich, *The Idea of the Book in the Middle Ages: Language Theory, Mythology, and Fiction* (Ithaca, N.Y.: Cornell Univ. Press, 1985), which came to hand after I had completed the present study. Gellrich's broad-ranging book addresses many of the issues I too regard as fundamental to an understanding of medieval poetics.

9. Gordon Leff, *The Dissolution of the Medieval Outlook: An Essay on Intellectual and Spiritual Change in the Fourteenth Century* (New York: New York Univ. Press, 1976), pp. 10–11. Laurence Eldredge has written a series of articles relating works of Chaucer to the nominalist ferment of the period: "Chaucer's *Hous of Fame* and the *Via Moderna,*" *Neuphilologische Mitteilungen* 71 (1970): 105–19; "Poetry and Philosophy in the *Parlement of Foules,*" *Revue de l'Univer-*

Leff observes further that these profound changes produced a "new openness which complemented the loss of system involved in the redrawing of conceptual boundaries" (p. 11).

Men of letters also participated in these changes. Paradoxically the *via moderna* of the new surge of vernacular literature led back to the *via classica* and the renewal of pagan, mainly Ciceronian, rhetoric. In the rhetorical view, derived from antiquity, language is a medium distinct from its referent and capable of systematic cultivation and systemization. This essentially pagan conception became an intellectual commonplace in the late Middle Ages, advanced by the humanist movement and the reassessment of classical culture. It is implicit in the familiar metaphor of language as a veil or garment, as expressed, for example, by the twelfth-century rhetorician Geoffrey of Vinsauf: "Although the meaning is one, let it not come content with one set of apparel. Let it vary its robes and assume different raiment." [10] Geoffrey's distinction between meaning and the verbal garment woven to adorn it relates to the ancient controversy between poetry and philosophy revived by the humanists of the late Middle Ages. Boccaccio, for example, argues in defense of poetry that it "adorns the whole composition with unusual interweaving of words and thoughts; and thus it veils truth in a fair and fitting garment of fiction." [11] From a rhetorical point of view the essential feature of this binary relation is the status it accords to language. Language is not fused with its object as realist doctrine, in both its Augustinian and its Jamesian versions, would have it. On the contrary, it is independent and palpable, a material to

---

sité d'Ottawa 40 (1970): 441–59; "Boethian Epistemology and Chaucer's *Troilus* in the Light of Fourteenth-Century Thought," *Mediaevalia* 2 (1976): 49–75. For a further elucidation of the significance of nominalist epistemology for our understanding of Chaucer's poetics see Larry Sklute, *Virtue of Necessity: Inconclusiveness and Narrative Form in Chaucer's Poetry* (Columbus: Ohio State Univ. Press, 1984), pp. 13–22. See also Russell Peck, "Chaucer and the Nominalist Questions," *Speculum* 53 (1978): 745–60.

10. Geoffrey of Vinsauf, *Poetria nova*, trans. Margaret F. Nims (Toronto: Pontifical Institute of Medieval Studies, 1967), p. 24.

11. *Boccaccio on Poetry, Being the Preface and the Fourteenth and Fifteenth Books of Boccaccio's "Genealogia deorum gentilium,"* trans. C. G. Osgood (Indianapolis, Ind.: Bobbs-Merrill, 1956), p. 39.

be "woven" and adorned, or as Geoffrey of Vinsauf regards it in another metaphor, it is "material to be moulded, like the moulding of wax" (p. 23). From this view of language it follows that the writer is one who exercises judgment and skill in choosing, shaping, and composing verbal materials. But since human choice inevitably introduces a dimension of arbitrariness, the question or correctness—or truth—is always open. The rhetor is an ambiguous authority.

Rhetoric in this sense was well established in the medieval curriculum, and it was familiar to educated men of letters. But as a subject of theoretical inquiry it did not fare as well as studies in logic, where the main advances of the nominalist movement took place. None of the so-called theorists, such as Geoffrey of Vinsauf, developed a consistent critical sense of the implications for *poetria nova* of the view that language is an arbitrary medium, managed by humans. They formulated no poetics, no theory of literature based on rhetorical principles, only prescriptive compositional techniques. Thoughtful poets such as Dante, Boccaccio, and Chaucer show evidence of an inchoate poetics, and Chaucer's dream visions address most of the fundamental issues, obliquely if not directly, as we shall see. But in the fourteenth century the new interest in language analysis produced theoretical advances in philosophy, particularly in logic, not in literary studies.

The beginnings of theoretical studies aimed at discovering what Todorov calls "principles of literariness" had to await the rehabilitation of rhetoric in modern times. Thanks to recent developments in literary theory, the values and possibilities of a rhetorical poetics are now widely appreciated and have had some notable impact on Chaucer studies as well. But during the first five or six decades of this century, which saw the production of a large body of influential Chaucer criticism, the dominant analytical model was distinctly Jamesian and "organic."[12]

---

12. Enshrined in one of the sacred texts of the New Criticism, under the rubric "The Organic Nature of Poetry," is the following statement of dogma: "The relationship among the elements in a poem is what is all important; it is not a mechanical relationship but one which is far more intimate and funda-

The critical event for modern theory was the rediscovery of the medieval, nonorganic view of language as a palpable medium, a "material to be moulded, like the moulding of wax," an autonomous medium or system to be distinguished from its referents. This view was first proposed in modern times by Ferdinand de Saussure in linguistics and applied in literary analysis by the Russian Formalists and the Prague School. It goes by many names and has been enlarged and refined in a diverse and often arcane terminology, but in its simplest form it is Saussure's differentiation between signifier (*signifiant*) and signified (*signifié*). The bridge between Saussure's linguistics and literary theory was established mainly by Slavic theorists, perhaps most influentially by Roman Jakobson, whose distinction between poetic language and its denoted object will sound familiar to students of medieval rhetoric: "The distinctive feature of poetry lies in the fact that a word is perceived as a word and not merely a proxy for the denoted object or an outburst of an emotion, that words and their arrangement, their meaning, their outward and inward form acquire weight and value of their own." [13] Similarly, in seeking to define the "literariness" of the novel, Formalist critics stressed the autonomous value of verbal structures and thus challenged the prevailing Symbolist and Jamesian doctrine of the inseparability of form and content. The analytical separation of language from its object was a new and fruitful proposition in 1915, the

---

mental. If we must compare a poem to the make-up of some physical object it ought not to be to a wall but to something organic like a plant" (Cleanth Brooks and Robert Penn Warren, *Understanding Poetry*, 3d ed. [New York: Holt, Rinehart and Winston, 1960], p. 16). This is essentially the same poetics that Henry James articulated for fiction.

13. Cited in Victor Erlich, *Russian Formalism: History, Doctrine*, 3d ed. (The Hague: Mouton, 1969), p. 183. Further to the relation between Saussurean linguistics and Formalist literary theory see Peter Steiner, *Russian Formalism: A Metapoetics* (Ithaca, N.Y.: Cornell Univ. Press, 1984), esp. pp. 208–10, 254–57. For an understanding of these developments and linkages with postmodernist theory the following are useful guides: Fredric Jameson, *The Prison-House of Language* (Princeton, N.J.: Princeton Univ. Press, 1972); Jonathan Culler, *Structuralist Poetics* (Ithaca, N.Y.: Cornell Univ. Press, 1975); Terence Hawkes, *Structuralism and Semiotics* (Berkeley: Univ. of California Press, 1977).

year in which Saussure's *Cours de Linguistique Générale* was posthumously published. Like the nominalist movement in the fourteenth century, Saussure's work exerted a strong influence on the development of new avenues of intellectual investigation, such as the modern science of semiotics and the positivist movement in philosophy. It also influenced the development of the structuralist movement and the diverse streams of postmodernism. And it opened the way to the rehabilitation of rhetoric.

The Russian Formalists demonstrated the literary possibilities of a quantitative approach to the verbal medium. Their work, largely unknown in the West during the hegemony of the New Criticism, provided a theoretical defense for the aesthetic values of nonrealist literature. Victor Shklovsky's analysis of *Tristram Shandy* is the classic illustration of techniques and values antithetical to James's concept of the work as a "living organism."[14] What is living in Sterne's novel, as Shklovsky tells us, is not a metaphorical organism but an actual, lively, and visible authorial management of "blocks of language" (the notion so abhorrent to Henry James), a placement and displacement of pieces of story. "Baring the devices" in this way is itself a feature of the poetics of the work.

Modern rhetorical theory provides a conceptual framework and a vocabulary for the analysis I am undertaking in this book. Gérard Genette's refinement of the Formalist model illustrates a way of talking about the materials of literary composition as an order separable from the reality literature addresses, an order possessed of principles of "literariness."[15] Genette defines literature in three aspects: story (*histoire*), narrative (*récit*), and narrating (*narration*). For Genette's "story" I also use terms such as content, the "signified," imaginary world, and fictional characters and situations. For "narra-

14. Published in 1921, Victor Shklovsky's essay appears in translation as "Sterne's *Tristram Shandy:* Stylistic Commentary," in *Russian Formalist Criticism: Four Essays,* ed. Lee T. Lemon and Marion J. Reis (Lincoln: Univ. of Nebraska Press, 1965).

15. Gérard Genette, *Narrative Discourse: An Essay in Method,* trans. Jane E. Lewin (Ithaca, N.Y.: Cornell Univ. Press, 1980).

tive," which is in every sense the most central as well as the most broadly connotative term, I use such varying equivalents as text, discourse, signifier, composition, medium, rhetorical dimension. "Narrating," at best an awkward gerund, refers to an aspect that has become familiar to Chaucerians in the plethora of commentary on the Chaucerian persona. The term refers to the impulse of rhetorical fiction to objectify, often self-consciously, the circumstances of its own utterance and thus to foreground the activity of writing. As Genette observes, narrative is intermediary to story on the one hand and to the circumstances of its uttering (the "narrating") on the other. Though the three aspects are interdependent, narrative is the only one present on the page. It is the high-energy point at which the writer's pen and the reader's eye converge and through which the reader finds access to the imaginary world of the story and, in the opposite direction, to the real but implied world of the author's narrating.

Chaucerian narrative, in highlighting its textuality, its composed quality or "literariness," invites primary emphasis on the verbal medium. In many ways, and in varying degrees at different times, it renders the medium opaque and noticeable in contrast to the transparency cultivated by the realist poetics of Balzac and James, who would have the medium dissolve into the "reality" it evokes. For example, in the *House of Fame,* as we shall see in more detail in the next chapter, Chaucer treats thematically the epistemological issue that preoccupies the rhetorical writer and is inevitably prominent in his work. In deliberately raising the question of its own validity, rhetorical narrative explores its own nature and questions its relation to truth. It raises questions that realist fiction, concealing its devices, leaves unasked. Chaucerian narrative has this self-reflexiveness in common with the avant-garde fiction of our own day, a relationship we shall consider more fully in the next chapter.

Since the idea of self-reflexivity recurs frequently in my later discussions, I want to clarify here the scope of the term. It denotes an objectified relationship between the text and its author. A self-reflexive text stresses both its verbal autonomy and its contingent character as a product of its composer. It

draws attention to its intermediate status, as narrative, between story and narrating. By highlighting this disjunction, a
self-reflexive text compromises one of the cardinal principles
of realist poetics: it violates the continuity of the poetic imagination and openly invites us to suspend the suspension of
disbelief. A self-reflexive text expands beyond realism to include both illusion and dis-illusion. In contrast, a nonreflex-
ive text cultivates the illusion that narrative dissolves into
story; it ignores by poetic fiat, so to speak, the textuality of
the medium. Such an illusion of textlessness is cultivated
by Dickens, for example, when he exclaims in the preface to
Little Dorrit that in a walk about London he discovered the
very room where Little Dorrit was born.[16] A magnificent artificer who bent every effort to conceal artifice, Dickens fuses
story and narrating, to the exclusion of narrative, in his aim to
produce the illusion of history (he calls it biography) rather
than reveal the actuality of fictional art. In a superficially
similar situation in the General Prologue, Chaucer deliberately exploits the distance between author and story that Dickens seeks to diminish. Chaucer's claim that he was there in the
Tabard and on the road, faithfully recording the discourse of
the other pilgrims, is a deliberately ironic play on authorship.
It strikes a vein of humor that is distinctly uncongenial to the
realist imagination because it betrays what Henry James calls a
"sacred office" and commits the "terrible crime" of conceding
that fiction is only story.[17] Self-reflexivity appeals to our consciousness of textuality and artifice. A distinct textual feature, observable without resort to inference or interpretation,
it unites reader and writer in conscious awareness of both the
rhetorical reality and the illusionary magic of the narrative
text.

A somewhat divergent view of reflexivity has been argued
by David Aers.[18] In his discussion of Chaucer's "reflexive imagi-

16. Charles Dickens, *Little Dorrit*, ed. H. P. Sucksmith (Oxford: Clarendon
Press, 1979), p. lx.
17. James, "The Art of Fiction," p. 379.
18. David Aers, *Chaucer, Langland, and the Creative Imagination* (London:
Routledge and Kegan Paul, 1980), pp. 80–116.

nation" Aers associates reflexivity with story rather than with text; reflexivity thus becomes what the text is about rather than what it is. Aers observes that Chaucer is sensitive to the contingent nature of discourse and skeptical about the grounds of received authority, but he turns to the Pardoner and the Wife of Bath to illustrate his idea of reflexivity. In so doing he leaves poetics and enters the realm of interpretation, in Todorov's sense of the distinction. He notes that the Pardoner is aware of the manipulative character of his own practices, and that he "*needs* to express his reflexivity and his critical insights" and that the need "is a product of his humanity" (p. 101). Aers's subject thus becomes the interpretation of character, and he makes a provocative contribution to the large body of commentary on the character of the Pardoner. But discussion of the presence or absence of reflexivity in the outlooks of the Canterbury pilgrims—the Pardoner and the Wife of Bath have it, the Parson does not—begs the questions that rhetorical theory explores.

The assumption that fictional characters can enjoy a privileged status outside the language they utter belongs to a realist poetics, which accepts as a given the illusion that a fictional character possesses personal autonomy. Chaucer's poetics, although it contains and exploits the possibilities for such illusion, invites our attention to the larger and prior question of the nature of fictional illusion itself. This it does by textual self-reflexivity, which is a property of the medium, not of the story, and reflects directly on the labor of writing, the primary relationship between the author and the formal structures into which he casts his language. In the *Canterbury Tales* Chaucer is the only maker of the text. Rhetorical analysis regards the pilgrims primarily as voices that Chaucer inscribes into the language of his text and only secondarily as reified and, to varying extents, "rounded" characters. Some of those voices, such as those that constitute the character Chaucer names Pardoner, reflect views and assumptions about language that probably coincide with Chaucer's own, as Aers notes. But we shall find the primary evidence of Chaucer's views, of his poetics, not in the mouths or the heads of characters reified by interpretive criticism but in the verbal figures and formal structures of Chaucerian texts. The aim of rhetorical analysis is to explore the vital textual ground that mediates between the writer's mind and the imaginary world he projects for the reader's apprehension. Rather than plunge into the depths of interpretation, we shall find riches enough on Chaucer's verbal surface. The words of Italo Calvino's Mr. Palomar, uttered in a different context, provide wise counsel for the student of Chaucer's art: "It is only after you have come to know the surface of things that you can venture to seek what is underneath. But the surface of things is inexhaustible."[19]

Recent theoretical studies such as those I have been citing confirm the aesthetic and philosophical validity of a rhetorical poetics. The realist view of rhetoric as a deceptive or mechanical device, antipathetic to the sincerity and vitality of art, is no longer widely held. Few would agree today with Manly's assertion that "the task of the artist is not to pad his tales with rhetoric, but to conceive all the events and characters in the forms and activities of life."[20] In Chaucer Manly found what he and his generation valued in literature, which was the "forms and activities of life," not the "padding" of rhetoric. We of a later generation, living in the "postmodern" age, also see ourselves in Chaucer's plenitude. But what we see is different. Reflecting our own cultural and intellectual preoccupations, the following description of contemporary "metafiction" also defines a large area of the modern reader's critical interest in Chaucerian narrative: "a celebration of the power of the creative imagination together with an uncertainty about the validity of its representations; an extreme self-consciousness about language, literary form and the act of writing fictions; a pervasive insecurity about the relationship of fiction to reality; a parodic, playful, excessive or deceptively naive

---

19. Italo Calvino, *Mr. Palomar,* trans. William Weaver (San Diego: Harcourt Brace Jovanovich, 1985), p. 55.

20. John M. Manly, "Chaucer and the Rhetoricians," in *Chaucer Criticism: The "Canterbury Tales,"* ed. Richard J. Schoeck and Jerome Taylor (Notre Dame, Ind.: Notre Dame Univ. Press, 1960), p. 285 (first published in *Proceedings of the British Academy* 12 [1926]: 95–113).

style of writing."[21] Today's writers and readers share with Chaucer this ambiguous orientation toward the relation of words and things, language and "life." "Postmodern" writers—Barth, Calvino, Beckett, and a host of others—have reconditioned us to a poetics of uncertainty, where the givens are not unity and coherence but multiplicity and contingency. Living in our own age of dissolving verities, we have developed a philosophical and literary orientation that resembles Chaucer's in many fundamental respects and alerts us to aesthetic values not easily recognizable from a realist perspective. The philosopher Ernest Moody has drawn the comparison, observing the "many symptoms to indicate that our age of analysis has brought us to a point comparable to that of six hundred years ago, when the cosmological and metaphysical framework, within which philosophers had worked for a thousand years, had been dissolved beyond repair."[22] As in the late Middle Ages, vestiges of the old reality remain, but the dominant orientation is skeptical and experimental.

We have become more tolerant of the limits of language in capturing the "forms and activities of life" and more responsive to its vagaries as a perceptual instrument. And we have become more tolerant—not to say appreciative—of verbal artifice and virtuosity as the artful registration of a shifting, elusive reality. Pending the arrival of an era when literature can again undertake the task of interpreting a unified reality acknowledged by all, pending, that is, a new Augustinian synthesis or a new Copernican-Newtonian world-frame, we are coming to terms with the values of a multivalent and ambiguous reality and its literary correlatives of dissonance, collage, and discontinuity. The intellectual and moral fluidity of our time and the aesthetics of uncertainty reproduce to an appreciable extent the conditions of Chaucer's fourteenth century and orient us to the positive values of his rhetorical poetics.

21. Patricia Waugh, *Metafiction: The Theory and Practice of Self-Conscious Fiction* (London and New York: Methuen, 1984), p. 2. See also Albert J. Guerard, "Notes on the Rhetoric of Anti-realist Fiction," *TriQuarterly* 30 (1974), 3–50.
22. Ernest A. Moody, *Studies in Medieval Philosophy, Science, and Logic* (Berkeley: Univ. of California Press, 1975), p. 319.

Does our interest in verbal surfaces, in "realms of discourse [that] bang together," [23] mean that we are willing to sacrifice life and emotion for artifice and mere virtuosity? It is easy to fall into such dualistic thinking, as Manly did, and regard Chaucer as *either* a rhetorician *or* an artist. To reclaim the rhetorical is not to deny Chaucer's capacity to satisfy both rhetorical and realist presuppositions. A rhetorical reading of Chaucer does not dismiss life and feeling but rather redirects emphasis from the verisimilitude of realistic content and dramatized characters to the labor itself of writing and composing poetic narratives. Life and feeling are located not exclusively in imagined content but also on the actual verbal surfaces, where the living poet confronted the awesome challenge of converting what he knew and what he felt into the constraining forms of language.

The relation between verbal surface and illusionary content will occupy much of our investigation of Chaucerian narrative in the chapters that follow. Rhetorical analysis affords a view of that dynamic interplay that is inaccessible to a mode of interpretation that places definitive value on rendering the verbal surface transparent. Because realist interpretation presupposes verisimilitude as a criterion of value, it is disinclined to value the signs of the craftsman's hand, but as we will see, Chaucer does not allow us to forget for long that we are engaged with a work of the pen. A valid Chaucerian poetics must take account of the intellectual dimension of Chaucerian narrative and its undisguised self-consciousness about the making of make-believe.

23. This phrase from Annie Dillard's description of "modernist" fiction suggests parallels with Chaucerian practice and a common basis in a rhetorical poetics. *Living by Fiction* (New York: Harper and Row, 1983), p. 24. See pp. 47–48.

Writing about Writing

The *House of Fame*

The dream-vision form richly exemplifies the requirements and the possibilities of a rhetorical poetics. Chaucer's lifelong devotion to the form is evidence that he valued it, and yet modern readers do not come easily to terms with medieval dream visions. The pioneer modern critics had less to say about Chaucer's dream visions than about his more "realistic" works, though there have been efforts to interpret the disjointed collage of dream-vision narrative as a realistic representation of actual dream experience. But the analogy between disjointed dreams and disjointed narrative does not take us very far.[1] Although the realities of dream experience provide a possible source of explanation for the discontinuities of Chaucerian dream visions, dream psychology, medieval or modern, has little to tell us about a finely wrought narrative like Ceyx and Alcione in the *Book of the Duchess,* or a wonderfully articulate discourse on the physics of sound in the *House of Fame,* or an intricate, multivoiced debate about love in the *Parlement of Foules.* Whatever may have been the in-

---

1. A contrary view, in which realistic dream psychology is seen as a unifying artistic device, is argued by Constance B. Hieatt, *The Realism of Dream Visions* (The Hague: Mouton, 1967), pp. 67–88. But I concur in the view of D. W. Robertson, Jr., that the dream vision form is "certainly not conducive to dream 'realism' of the kind envisaged by Kittredge and Malone" (and Hieatt) ("*The Book of the Duchess,*" in *Companion to Chaucer Studies,* ed. Beryl Rowland, rev. ed. [New York: Oxford Univ. Press, 1979], p. 409). For a balanced view of the artistic and psychological elements of the dream-vision form see A. C. Spearing, *Medieval Dream-Poetry* (Cambridge: Cambridge Univ. Press, 1976), pp. 1–15, 48–110.

fluence of real dreaming, Chaucer modeled his dream visions on literary texts he knew, and although he was interested in dream psychology, his conception of it was derived from literary texts—mainly Macrobius—and was incorporated into his own textual collage as one of its many subjects. Chaucer's dream visions were neither imitations of real dreams nor accounts of visionary experience—which leaves little to be said for the generic term except that it is convenient.

In its early forms vision poetry was closely associated with the realities of religious experience. The Scriptural visions of Daniel and John were understood to participate in spiritual reality and to bring to the world important prophetic messages. That realist tradition, in which the written text bore the burden of spiritual truth, reached an apogee in the *Divine Comedy*, though not without benefit of an immensely complex literary artifice. But the *Romance of the Rose* radically diverted the ancient tradition, and it was this newly secularized mode, richly embellished with allusions to the Latin classics, that provided Chaucer with the models for his dream visions. These are rhetorical compositions whose principles of order find their basis not in the extrinsic realm of dream experience or visionary experience but in a poetics of textual collage, narrative self-reflexiveness, and stylistic flamboyance. The prominence of these features is not unrelated to the novelty of fourteenth-century English as a literary medium for compositions that aspired to the company Chaucer named in *Troilus and Criseyde* (v. 1792)—"Virgile, Ovide, Omer, Lucan, and Stace"—not to mention Jean de Meun, Dante, and Boccaccio.

In the dream visions Chaucer explored a range of generic forms and tonal registers that his vernacular had never before attempted. That such an enterprise should display a high degree of self-reflexiveness and some uncertainty about the role of poet and the relation of poetry to truth should occasion little surprise. At any rate, these features of the dream visions attract the interest of rhetorically oriented analysis and to a large extent establish the groundwork of Chaucer's poetics.

The *House of Fame* stands out among the dream visions in its preoccupation with questions about the validity of language and the nature of poetic composition. It addresses these issues explicitly, though not systematically or conclusively, and it also displays in its compositional structure evidence of a distinctly self-conscious, "experimental" orientation toward the uses of language. For these reasons it serves well as an introduction to Chaucer's poetics and as a reference point for further explorations among Chaucer's works.

Although it has always been regarded as one of Chaucer's most puzzling poems, critics now seem to agree that the *House of Fame* is in large part a statement about poetry.[2] That a poetic text could be about writing, about its own composition rather than about a depicted object or content, is, as we have seen, an idea whose time has come (again). It is a major preoccupation of modern fiction, and it creates a particular resonance in the *House of Fame*, whose manifest content is so diffuse and multifarious—a discussion of dream lore, a condensed version of the *Aeneid*, a disquisition on the physics of sound, and an extended personification allegory of Fame's court, to note only the highlights.

Certainly there is little here (and less, even, than the other dream visions offer) for the reader interested primarily in the story—in character and plot and their meaning. Criticism in the early years of this century, when social realism was the predominant mode of imaginative literature, had relatively little to say about the *House of Fame*. A work hardly worthy of the mature poet of the *Canterbury Tales*, the *House of Fame* was interpreted—in the realist pursuit of referentiality—as a bildungsroman of the poet's own progress—Chaucer turning from old models to real men, Chaucer disappointed in love

---

2. For a good statement of the prevailing view and a bibliography see Laurence K. Shook, *"The House of Fame,"* in Rowland, *Companion to Chaucer Studies*, pp. 414–27. Unfortunately Shook's bibliography omits one of the best treatments, and possibly the first, of the *House of Fame* as an essay in poetics, Robert O. Payne, *The Key of Remembrance: A Study of Chaucer's Poetics* (New Haven, Conn.: Yale Univ. Press, 1963), pp. 129–37. Further refinements of this view are offered by Robert B. Burlin, *Chaucerian Fiction* (Princeton, N.J.: Princeton Univ. Press, 1977), pp. 45–58, and Donald R. Howard, "Chaucer's Idea of an Idea," in *Essays and Studies 1976*, ed. E. T. Donaldson (Atlantic Highlands, N.J., 1976), pp. 39–55.

and turning away from the works of Venus, Chaucer maturing in the discovery of the transitoriness of fame.[3] From the same impulse came Manly's theory that Chaucer's poetic career "progressed" from rhetoric to realism. Since Manly's time Chaucerians have learned more respect for rhetoric and for the varied interests of *homo rhetoricus*. As a result of our relatively recent recognition of realism as a convention rather than the standard of literary value, we are better able to recognize the differing aesthetic values and epistemological implications of a rhetorical poetics and, in particular, a rhetorical poem such as the *House of Fame*.

Interest in the *House of Fame* as an art of poetry is related to the widespread interest today in the nature of writing as a human activity. Not only critics but writers themselves evince such an interest. The fiction that is usually designated postmodern or experimental or avant-garde—beginning with Joyce and including Nabokov, Borges, Beckett, Barth, Pynchon, and many others—is largely preoccupied with its own nature as fiction. It is largely preoccupied, that is to say, with the theoretical questions we have come to associate with the *House of Fame*.

Before turning to Chaucer's poem we shall consider, in a brief excursus, some modern rhetorical narratives—"metafictions" they are called in postmodernist parlance—whose counter-realist emphasis on verbal surfaces, mixed styles, and shifting perspectives will orient us to similar features of the *House of Fame*. The postmodernists' rejection of the old verities of recognizable characters, logical plots, and unambiguous meaning has produced an understandable resistance from readers and critics and has generated a critical climate of controversy and uncertainty in many ways analogous to the realist-nominalist situation in the fourteenth century. Whether or not we place a high value on language-oriented fiction of the twentieth century, modern "metafiction" can alert us to features of the *House of Fame* that realist-oriented fictions and

---

3. For an early dismissal of this view see W. O. Sypherd, *Studies in Chaucer's Hous of Fame* (1907; New York: Haskell House, 1965), pp. 15–16.

criticism tend to stigmatize or overlook. Conversely, the *House of Fame* can be seen to engage issues that many writers and critics find vitally important today.

Analysts of today's "new" fiction rarely recognize how old it is. Behind Annie Dillard's assessment of postrealist fiction, for example, a Chaucerian can see the *House of Fame* looming up as a silent progenitor: "The point of view shifts; the prose style shifts and its tone; characters turn into things; sequences of events abruptly vanish. Images clash; realms of discourse bang together. Zeus may order a margarita. . . . Nothing temporal, spatial, perceptual, social, or moral is fixed." [4] Dillard acknowledges some historical affinities when she comments that "Joyce, 163 years after Sterne, started breaking the narrative in *Ulysses*" (p. 22). But to my knowledge the only study of contemporary fiction with sufficient historical range to recognize the affinity with Chaucerian poetics is Gabriel Josipovici's *The World and the Book*. [5]

Josipovici stresses Chaucer's preoccupation with the puzzling relation between imagination and truth and the problematic validity of language. For a poet whose "primary concern is with the truth . . . the first truth to set out is that the poem is not truth but an invention of his own" (p. 81). Josipovici reminds us that the signs of Chaucer's self-awareness as a storyteller, a craftsman of language, are important to our understanding of the poetry, as important as his characters and plots and the inevitably tendentious interpretations they evoke. The act of telling is tendentious enough; the nature of its relation to experience is the overwhelming question. Acute consciousness of language and of his own role as an artisan of language, a rhetor, unites today's avant-garde writer with Chaucer in a mutual dissociation from the realist's assumption that truth is unambiguously accessible through language.

As Hugh Kenner observes, Joyce was the critical figure in

---

4. Annie Dillard, *Living by Fiction* (New York: Harper and Row, 1983), p. 24.

5. Gabriel Josipovici, *The World and the Book: A Study of Modern Fiction* (London: Macmillan, 1971), p. 302.

the postmodernist revolt against the hegemony of objectivity. Since Sprat's Royal Society and Defoe, rhetoric had been stigmatized as at best superfluous and at worst dishonest, the antithesis of plain, objective truth, both in the language of fiction and in that of public (and private) affairs. *Ulysses* is significant as "the decisive English-language book of the century" because of Joyce's revolutionary (or, historically speaking, reactionary) attitude toward language.[6] From its beginning in "objective" naturalism *Ulysses* moves through an "unfolding of styles" to end in parody, the only possible end of naturalism, as Kenner points out. Joyce's artful enactment of literary history demonstrates that language is not neutral, that naturalism is not the ultimate or the complete style of fiction, and that *Ulysses* is about the infinite resources of language as much as it is about Dublin or Leopold Bloom or Stephen or the *Odyssey*.

Renewed respect for the verbal medium itself—by which I mean an appreciation of its aesthetic possibilities as well as a sophisticated skepticism about its reliability as an instrument of perception—has brought into question the measurement of the quality of fiction by its truth to life. Postmodern writers and much contemporary criticism question the meaning of both terms, art and life, and ask whether Beckett's or Nabokov's fiction is any less "true to life" than the fiction of so-called social realism. The overwhelming questions are epistemological: true to whose life, observed by whom, with what predispositions, from what vantage point? More fundamentally, is the literary object life observed or life observing? Is the fiction "about" an objective reality, or is it about the act of observing, the act of writing, of translating vision and audition, thought and feeling into words and sentences and books?[7]

6. Hugh Kenner, *Joyce's Voices* (Berkeley: Univ. of California Press, 1978), p. xii. On the seventeenth-century origins of the decline of rhetoric see also Josipovici, pp. 142–49.

7. One must decide the extent of one's agreement on this issue as it relates to Chaucer studies. I am sympathetic with Martin Stevens's view that realism "now has ceased to exist as a mode of interpretation to be reckoned with" in Chaucer criticism ("Chaucer and Modernism," in *Chaucer at Albany,*

Solipsism has become an inevitable feature of our outlook, in which the viewer's mind and the medium of perception define the "objective" world subjectively. The art historian E. H. Gombrich's observation that there is no such thing as a neutral naturalism is consistent with the physicist Werner Heisenberg's uncertainty principle and the point that the act of viewing and the instrument of viewing alter the object. The instrument of viewing for writers is of course language.

Always close to the surface of Samuel Beckett's fiction is the question whether he is writing about the world or writing about writing about the world. The following passage, from the first of four stories the speaker in *Malone Dies* proposes to tell himself for his own amusement, illustrates the self-consciousness of the writer about style and idiom and also his anxiety about the troublesome arbitrariness of fiction.

> I have tried to reflect on the beginning of my story. There are things I do not understand. But nothing to signify. I can go on.
> Sapo had no friends—no, that won't do.
> Sapo was on good terms with his little friends, though they did not exactly love him. The dolt is seldom solitary. He boxed and wrestled well, was fleet of foot, sneered at his teachers and sometimes even gave them impertinent answers. Fleet of foot? Well well.[8]

Beckett is here writing about a writer (or teller) reflecting on the meaning—or the meaninglessness—of his art. Does it matter, we are invited to ask, whether or not Sapo had friends? And "fleet of foot," fine language indeed, but is the idiom of Butcher-Lang's Homer better or truer than "fast runner" for our Sapo? Or why not "slow and clumsy"? Malone's dialogue

---

ed. Rossell Hope Robbins [New York: Burt Franklin, 1975], p. 200). But the appearance of Charles A. Owen, *Pilgrimage and Storytelling in the "Canterbury Tales": The Dialectic of "Ernest" and "Game"* (Norman: Univ. of Oklahoma Press, 1977), suggests that Stevens's dictum is premature. For a socio-ideologically oriented essay that relates Chaucer to some recent French nonrealist criticism see Stephen Knight, "Chaucer and the Sociology of Literature," *Studies in the Age of Chaucer* 2 (1980): 15–51.

8. Samuel Beckett, *Malloy, Malone Dies, and The Unnamable: Three Novels by Samuel Beckett* (New York: Grove Press, 1959), p. 258.

with himself as he oscillates between the roles of author and narrator is about the power of language arbitrarily to endow its object with one quality or another—good fame or ill.

In implying these questions Beckett explores the gap between language and objective reality and discovers that the observed object or character lives in the language of the observing subject, not in an essence that the writer seeks to make speak. Beckett finds a cosmic humor and irony in this disjunction between objective reality and human language. In foregrounding the problem, Beckett reflects an uneasy ambivalence about a medium that is both powerless to reach objective truth and powerfully persuasive. We will find evidence that Chaucer shares this ambivalent state of mind about his art.

The act of writing is similarly subjected to multileveled solipsistic analysis throughout the works of John Barth, wherein the role of the writer subsumes the distinction between subject and object. What is the fiction entitled "Title" about—or is it a fiction? Set somewhat past the middle of the series of fictions in the book entitled *Lost in the Funhouse*, "Title" begins:

> Beginning: in the middle, past the middle, nearer three-quarters done, waiting for the end. Consider how dreadful so far: passionless, abstraction, pro, dis. And it will get worse. Can we possibly continue?
>
> Plot and theme: notions vitiated by this hour of the world but as yet not successfully succeeded. Conflict, complication, no climax. . . .

and it ends, seven pages later, in mid-sentence:

> Oh God comma I abhor self-consciousness. I despise what we have come to; I loathe our loathesome loathing, our place our time our situation, our loathsome art, this ditto necessary story. The blank of our lives. It's about over. Let the *denouement* be soon and unexpected, painless if possible, quick at least, above all soon. Now now! How in the world will it ever[9]

9. John Barth, *Lost in the Funhouse* (New York: Bantam Books, 1969), pp. 102, 110.

Barth—or is it Barth?—undertakes to clarify "Title" in a prefatory note, complete as follows:

> The triply schizoid monologue entitled "Title" addresses itself simultaneously to three matters: the "Author's" difficulties with his companion, his analogous difficulties with the story he's in process of composing, and the not dissimilar straits in which, I think mistakenly, he imagines his culture and its literature to be. In the stereophonic performance version of the story, the two "sides" debate—in identical authorial voice, as it is after all a *monologue intérieur*—across the twin channels of stereo tape, while the live author, like Mr. Interlocutor between Tambo and Bones in the old showboat-shows, supplies such self-interrupting and self-censoring passages as "Title" and "fill in the blank"—relinquishing his role to the auditor at the. (pp. x–xi)

For Barth fiction is an instrumentality in the profoundly problematic act of perception. In his fiction the labor of writing is never far from the center of attention, sometimes overwhelming the fiction and its maker as well.

Perhaps the classic statement of the modern writer's dilemma of role is Jorge Luis Borges's story "Borges and Myself." Commenting on this pithy tour de force, Borges states, "A preoccupation with identity and sometimes its discord, duality, runs through much of my work." [10] Certainly "Borges and Myself" demonstrates the point as it articulates with simple lucidity that complex relationship: "I live, I let myself live, so that Borges can weave his tales and poems, and those tales and poems are my justification." The piece ends with the only possible answer to the unanswerable question: "Which of us is writing this page I don't know."

Such is the preoccupation and the predicament of the writer in the modern world. The central issues are not plot and character but language, perception, and the role and position of the writer in the textual nexus of the world, his audience, and himself. Whatever the resolution of these problems may be, these are the issues that the contemporary writer confronts

10. Jorge Luis Borges, *The Aleph and Other Stories, 1933–1969*, ed. and trans. Norman Thomas di Giovanni (New York: Dutton, 1978), p. 277.

and places before us as both the subject and object of fiction. Painfully aware that his language is the only reality he has, the contemporary novelist can no longer express "meaning" in the old objective sense: rather he displays himself in the solipsistic activity of writing.

Let us conclude this excursus with a brief look at an example of realist fiction, whose antirhetorical orientation contrasts instructively both with contemporary practice and with the practice of Chaucer. The opening sentences of *The Golden Bowl*, a masterpiece of realist fiction, reveal attitudes toward language and authorial identity strikingly antithetical to those displayed in the "experimental" illustrations considered above:

> The Prince had always liked his London, when it had come to him; he was one of the modern Romans who find by the Thames a more convincing image of the truth of the ancient state than any they have left by the Tiber. Brought up on the legend of the City to which the world paid tribute, he recognized in the present London much more than in contemporary Rome the real dimensions of such a case. If it was a question of an *Imperium*, he said to himself, and if one wished, as a Roman, to recover a little the sense of that, the place to do so was on London Bridge, or even, on a fine afternoon in May, at Hyde Park Corner.[11]

Precisely and delicately fashioned as they are, these sentences are designed for transparency, to focus the reader's attention not on themselves but directly and intently on the object. That the object, the Prince, is presented "subjectively," by way of his inner consciousness, does not alter the objectivity of the presentation. Such a mode of narration aims to place the reader in the utmost proximity to the object—whether that object be a human consciousness or a natural landscape. Too opaque a medium would interfere with such intimacy by breaking the illusion of presence at the scene. Essential to the reader's illusion of presence is the illusion of the author's absence. Paradoxically, James's mastery of the resources of language is bent to the aim of concealing an authorial part in the

11. Henry James, *The Golden Bowl* (New York: Charles Scribner's Sons, 1925), p. 3.

fiction. The illusion is that of a seamless conjunction with reality: the fiction is not made, but flows ineluctably from reality. The definite article, used with the indefinite identification of the character—the Prince—produces the illusion of previous and continuing familiarity in a continuity between reality and fiction that is not broken by the beginning of the book.

Such, then, are the essential features of a realist poetics. A considerable amount of Chaucer interpretation has been based on the realist requirement that the language of fiction appear to emanate from the object rather than from the mind of a rhetor. That Chaucer could respond so well to such an approach is a tribute to the range of his artistry, but as we shall see in a later chapter, even his most objective renderings of character and situation are effectively shaped by rhetorical considerations. The *House of Fame* has always responded poorly to realist interpretation. It is a relatively pure example of rhetorical composition, whose aim is not truth but persuasive discourse. Unlike *Troilus* and much of the *Canterbury Tales*, it offers very little objectified content. In highlighting language and the craft of the maker (as well as his ambivalence toward his craft), the *House of Fame* appeals to the interests of *homo rhetoricus.* Although realistic narrative—with coherent plot, "believable" characters, and recognizable setting—will always exert its spell, a different kind of narrative directs awareness to the verbal surface that mediates between object and subject. It is on this surface that the writer has faced his blank page and created an instrument of perception, and it is here that the reader's mind converges with the writer's. Critical interest today focuses on these points of intersection where the fundamental energies of composition are registered. To this interest the *House of Fame* responds very well.

Despite the considerable agreement today that the *House of Fame* is a statement about poetry, certain critical distinctions must be drawn. In particular we need to distinguish between thematic and structural or formal applications of the *ars poetica* idea. As a unifying theme *ars poetica* is only somewhat more satisfactory than other thematic proposals, such as love, renown, autobiography, Dantesque eschatology, Boethian felicity, and so forth, all of which evolve from the primary assumption that the poem exists to convey meanings about objective reality. I do not mean to suggest that "poetry" is not *a* thematic concern. Explicitly broached in the well-noted reference to "art poetical" in the invocation to book 3 the subject is equally evident in less explicit passages, such as the manifold allusions to classical poets and their works. There is also a connection, drawn by the Eagle, between the love poems "Geffrey" has composed and the visit to the house of Fame, which Jove provides as a reward to enlarge the poet's vision. The poem is indeed about poetry, and in some sense it is about the growth and education of a poet, perhaps even Geoffrey Chaucer.

But there are many reasons why such a thematic interpretation is unsatisfactory. Like the thematic interpretation of any literary work, it formulates an extraliterary proposition of a very general sort and fails to account for the "feel" of a work, its "literariness," its unique form and body. To regard "poetry" as the theme of the *House of Fame* is justifiable so long as we treat such an observation as a beginning rather than a conclusion. In fact the *House of Fame* probably possesses more thematic continuity than either the *Book of the Duchess* or the *Parlement of Foules.*[12] The Eagle's disquisition on sound waves and their relation to poetry and fame can be interpreted as something of a tour de force in rationalizing such a continuity. But finally I think we must recognize how little thematic continuity tells us about this poem. However firm or fragile we may deem the thematic thread to be, the poem is more disjunct and disparate than continuous and integrated.

The Eagle's speech, for example, is both more and less than a subordinate contribution to a theme. Digressive and disproportionate as it is, this part of the poem, like many of its other parts, assumes a character of its own. The Eagle is a major figure in the poem. He speaks of many things, though mainly the physics of sound, and in his pedantry, his pomposity, and his narrow literal-mindedness he is the center of

---

12. In saying this I revise my earlier estimate of the *House of Fame*, hazarded in "The Compositional Structure of the *Book of the Duchess,*" *Chaucer Review* 9 (1974): 102.

compelling dramatic and satiric forces. A similar variety of interests is generated by each of the other major parts of the narrative, the Aeneas story and the figurative depictions of Fame's palace and the house of Rumor. To mine these rich veins for traces of a single theme is an exercise in prodigality, not to say pedantry, of the kind Chaucer was so ready to deride. As a thematic key to a poem that has so long eluded unitary interpretation, *ars poetica* is as reductive as any other, and reductive interpretation seems especially inappropriate for a poem so obviously expansive and encyclopedic. Poetry assumes a place—jostles for a place, one might say—among the many subjects of this poem: dreams, love, fame, auditory physics, cosmology, mythology, epistemology. The very profusion of subjects, what one critic calls a "troublesome abundance of material,"[13] stands squarely in the way of the otherwise attractive hypothesis that poetry is the thematic center of the *House of Fame*.

Another difficulty with the quest for a unifying theme is that the poem treats all of its many subjects with equal skepticism and irony or parody. This is the point that Sheila Delany develops to the logical conclusion that the thematic center of the poem is the absence of fixity and that therefore meaning is to be sought not in thematic development or a statement about something but in method or structure, particularly the "Gothic" method of structural repetition.[14]

13. Burlin, *Chaucerian Fiction*, p. 46. It is worth noting that "troublesome abundance" is a feature of Chaucerian practice in characterization as well as theme. The variety of character types in the *House of Fame*—legendary personages; a talking eagle; the crowds of legendary, historical, and contemporary people surging through the halls of Fame's palace; the personified Fame herself; the inconspicuously naturalistic "frend" who directs Geffrey to the house of Rumor—suggests the variety of character types employed by Chaucer in his art at large. For an appreciation of Chaucer's range and virtuosity in this respect, in contrast with the "single octave" available to realist authors, see Bertrand H. Bronson, *In Search of Chaucer* (Toronto: Univ. of Toronto Press, 1960), pp. 24–25.

14. Sheila Delany, *Chaucer's "House of Fame": The Poetics of Skeptical Fideism* (Chicago: Univ. of Chicago Press, 1972), pp. 49, 67, 76, and passim. John Fyler sees absence of fixity as a palpable theme in "the imperfections of authority, experience, and the human mind that attempts by balancing them to make sense of things" (*Chaucer and Ovid* [New Haven, Conn.: Yale Univ. Press, 1979], p. 23).

Even "art poetical" is treated ironically as Chaucer depicts
journeyman Geffrey disclaiming it in favor of "o sentence":

> Nat that I wilne, for maistrye,
> Here art poetical be shewed;
> . . . .
> And that I do no diligence
> To shewe craft, but o sentence.
> (1094–1100)

In thus parodying the writer who thinks he can avoid "craft"
and simply write truth, Chaucer demonstrates his familiarity
with the dilemma that today's "experimental" writers have
rediscovered.

Skepticism, irony, and parody undermine certainty about
the meaning of narrated events. Seeing nothing unambiguously, the reader continually reevaluates the narrative. The
Aeneas and Dido story presents the hero as an exemplar of
public duty, and it condemns him for personal infidelity. The
Eagle's disquisition on Aristotelian physics is derided by its
own pomposity. The poem fairly bristles with antinomies. Finally it presents poetry and its own language in a problematic
light.

The opening of the *House of Fame* illustrates Chaucer's
method. The speaker's extensive preamble to the account of his
wonderful dream—some 120 lines of digressive talk, largely
about himself—fixes our awareness on that speaking voice. In
effect Chaucer objectifies the labor of composition and locates
it in a dimension "above" the dream events to be recounted.
This is the manner of self-reflexive narrative, quantifying the
medium and drawing attention to the presence of language,
in contrast to the realist effort to achieve medial transparency.
Chaucer's Geffrey is a confrere of Beckett's Malone and Barth's
Ambrose, whose prominence foregrounds the laborer with
language, struggling against the inevitable arbitrariness of his
medium and its limited capacity to record the truth of experience. Geffrey addresses several matters, including the nature
and causes of dreams, but especially the problems of writing,
of transmitting experience through language. As he demonstrates, writing, or "telling," is a difficult business that one
sets about only with due deliberation and ritual. Chaucer's

display of his speaker's preparations, including his adver-
tisements for himself ("Ne no man elles me beforn, / Mette
. . . / So wonderful a drem as I" [ll. 60–61]), his prayer to the
god of sleep for help in recounting his dream accurately
("And to this god, that I of rede, / Prey I that he wol me
spede / My sweven for to telle aryght" [ll. 77–79]), and his
curse for those who might misconstrue his account (as well as
his blessing for those who "tak hit wel"), is humorous in its
parody of self-conscious rhetorical composition. Chaucer employs great skill and tact in depicting a protagonist struggling
tactlessly, with little sense of proportion or propriety, to tell
the truth of his dream experience.

Prolixity, a major problem for this earnest teller, is at the
same time a major resource for Chaucer. In depicting a speaker
engrossed in the formalities of good writing, Chaucer exploits
the conventions of the dream-vision form and the methods of
amplification prescribed by the rhetorical handbooks. In particular, he appears to heed Geoffrey of Vinsauf's advice on
amplification, or "travelling the more spacious route": "Do
not let your words move straight onward through the subject,
but, circling it, take a long and winding path around what you
were going to say briefly. Retard the tempo by thus increasing
the number of words."[15] After the opening entreaty (*exclama-
tio*)—"God turne us every drem to goode!"—which is repeated (*expolitio*) fifty-eight lines later, the narrator gives a
conventional account of dream lore (though uniquely Chaucerian in its archness and its idiom), followed by a disclaimer
of any personal understanding of such matter. And again, following immediately on this opening diversion comes another.
Between the stated intention now "to tellen everydel" of his
wonderful dream of December 10 (ll. 59–65) and the act of
doing so falls a lengthy shadow. Not until line 111, which repeats the December date of line 63, does the speaker manage
to address his announced purpose. The repeated line frames
the digression and signals its completion as a textual segment.

15. Geoffrey of Vinsauf, *Poetria nova*, trans. Margaret F. Nims (Toronto:
Pontifical Institute of Medieval Studies, 1967), pp. 24, 25.

Chaucer employs subtler means as well to highlight and parody the writer struggling to control his material. For example, after praying God to grant to all sympathetic listeners of his tale "for to stonden alle in grace / Of her loves," the teller cannot let well enough alone but must add the bathetic "or in what place / That hem were levest for to stonde" (ll. 85–87). A similar touch of the bathos occurs with the rhyme on the word God in this passage (which also illustrates the speaker's capacity for overstatement):

> And whoso thorgh presumpcion,
> Or hate, or skorn, or thorgh envye,
> Dispit, or jape, or vilanye,
> Mysdeme hyt, pray I Jesus God
> That (dreme he barefot, dreme he shod),
> That every harm that any man
> Hath had, syth the world began
> Befalle hym thereof, or he sterve.
>
> (94–101)

The gratuitous allusion to the hypothetical reader-dreamer's state of dress not only produces an irreverent rhyme but also displays a lack of sensitivity to literary propriety and continuity of mood. The ineptitude is the narrator's, the humor Chaucer's. This complex effect depends on Chaucer's sense of the gap between experience and its verbal rendering. It also depends on the deftness of his handling of the ironies of that relation.

As an element of Chaucer's rhetorical play, the digressiveness and prolixity of this matter prefatory to the dream itself are of course an elaborate pretense. Unlike the realist author, who simply pretends (as in the relation between Dickens and Little Dorrit noted earlier), Chaucer builds the *act* of pretending into his verbal structure. Chaucer objectifies his pretense mainly by parodic excess, which renders the presentational voice ambiguous and not plainly identifiable with the author. This built-in uncertainty and focal ambivalence disconcerts *homo seriousus*, who, like Manly, devalues such passages by taking them too seriously as "padding" and fails to recognize that rhetorical pretense—the playing and displaying of roles—is a high literary value, not a sign of ineptitude and obtuseness.

When we look to the poem as a literary composition by Chaucer rather than a presentation by a struggling and inept (though engaging) dream teller, we recognize that the presentational level is in fact an element of the poem whose literary status equals that of the "story," or content of the dream. The latter is the pretended substance, while the telling is presented as persiflage. Together they constitute the ironic rhetorical mode of the poem. This mixture of viewpoints and styles proves troublesome to the realist critic, who is predisposed toward continuity and Jamesian homogeneousness of texture and who might be inclined to apologize for such "irregularities" or to overlook them entirely in his desire for an unmediated immersion in story.

By directing our awareness to the disjunction between story and narrative (or *histoire* and *récit*, past events and present telling), Chaucer maintains the shifting perspective characteristic of self-reflexive narrative. The *House of Fame* exhibits other forms of discontinuity as well. In fact, contrary to the aesthetic presuppositions of many modern readers, structural and thematic discontinuity are essential and positive features of the poem. Structural discontinuity, in narrative collage or the juxtaposition of largely self-sufficient segments or blocks of discourse, is most plainly apparent among the larger divisions of content. A summary of the *Aeneid*, a disquisition on the physics of sound, and a long exposition of the workings of the Lady Fame constitute a diversified assortment of materials. They differ not only in size but also in shape and genre. Although the poem as a whole may be regarded as a narrative for lack of a better term—Chaucer was no generic purist—the Aeneas and Dido story is the only one of the three major sections of the poem that is a narrative, more or less properly so called. The Eagle's discourse on sound is a piece of argumentative rhetoric (self-parodying, to be sure), and the bulk of book 3 is a lavishly detailed personification allegory. Such extreme differentiation in content and generic mode tends to individuate these parts in the form of large blocks of composition, strung loosely together on the thin strand of the protagonist's narrating discourse.

Chaucer further emphasizes the demarcations by rhetorical means. The Aeneas story, for example, as William Joyner has pointed out,[16] is framed by a pair of closely matched descriptions of the temple of Venus (ll. 120–27, 468–73), which surround the condensed story with two descriptions of the same material, delivered in the same awestruck tone, and with much of the same language. These ornamental "bookends" not only set off the epic story from the rest of the poem but also display the artist's hand, "moulding his material like the moulding of wax," as enjoined in the *Poetria nova*. They also illustrate Geoffrey of Vinsauf's first method of amplification, *expolitio*, which is to "reiterate, in a number of clauses, a single thought."[17] This explicit and often exaggerated structuring results in an irregular, spasmodic movement of the narrative that is quite contrary to the realist criterion of homogeneous texture and smooth, "natural" flow.

Rhetorical impairment of the narrative flow occurs throughout the poem, articulating small units as well as large ones. Within the Aeneas story, for example, Joyner notes sixteen separate "narrative panels," each delineated by "Ther sawgh I" or a similar pseudo-authorial phrase external to the narrative proper. Similarly he finds that in book 2 "The dreamer's account of his adventure with the Eagle is also set out in a series of well-defined segments—the description of the desert, the story of the flight, the ecphrasis of the palace of Fame, etc." (p. 6). In the same manner the judgment of Fame in book 3, which Delany designates as an "allegorical set piece,"[18] divides itself by explicit numbers into a sequence of nine tableaux of petitioners. This ninefold *expolitio* amplifies its basic idea with dazzling rhetorical bravura. As a set of variations on a theme this is a rhetorical tour de force, comparable in the

---

16. William Joyner, "Parallel Journeys in Chaucer's *House of Fame*," *Papers in Language and Literature* 12 (1976): 5–6.

17. Geoffrey of Vinsauf, pp. 23–24.

18. Delany, *Chaucer's "House of Fame,"* p. 104.

color, variety, and vigor of its language to the memorable descriptions of the opposing armies in the Knight's Tale. Though the idea of fame's arbitrariness is present throughout, it is overwhelmed by the sheer splendor of this set piece. The visual and auditory imagery of the procession of Fame's petitioners displays the English language in a range of expressiveness rarely matched, before Chaucer or after.

The transitional passage that immediately follows the procession of Fame's petitioners and defines the end of that segment of the poem is especially interesting for what it reveals about Chaucer's compositional method and his idea of structure. Following the final blast of Aeolus's black trumpet, the focus shifts abruptly to the speaker—"With that y gan aboute wende" (l. 1868)—as he turns to address the nameless "Frend" who happens conveniently to be standing there, conveniently, that is, for Chaucer's compositional purposes. The outcome of their exchange is the news that the narrator is in the wrong place. Continuity has broken down, again. Chaucer does not conceal that he has indulged in a grand digression, a splendid irrelevance, and left his protagonist to complain that "these be no suche tydynges / As I mene of" (ll. 1894–95). He has always known—"Sith that first y hadde wit"—about fame. Where, he asks—apparently with some impatience, though he had shown none during the exhaustive display of Fame's doings—where are the promised tidings of love or other such glad things? Plainly Chaucer's protagonist has profited little. He is lost in the house of Fame. He is bewildered by what he learns about fame's tidings, which he finds to be but words on the wind, arbitrarily uttered and preserved or lost by the accidents of history. The explicit preoccupation with language in these passages momentarily brings together protagonist and author, sharing awe as well as bewilderment over the power of language and its duplicity. Chaucer would have appreciated John Barth's haunting metaphor, in which the fiction is subsumed in the foregrounded process of making it; the protagonist in Barth's fictional funhouse becomes the author lost in the verbal matrix of his own making: "He wishes he had never entered the funhouse. But he has. Then he wishes he were dead. But he's not. Therefore he will construct funhouses for others and be their secret operator—though he would rather be among the lovers for whom funhouses are designed" (p. 94). This is a supremely Chaucerian figure for one who knows nothing of love himself, or of writing, but is condemned to the role of poet, servant of the servants of love.

Having completed his treatment of Fame's palace, Chaucer employs the arbitrary device of Geffrey's "Frend," the intermediary from nowhere, to move the poem to the next set piece, on the house of Rumor. Here too meaning is secondary to verbal brilliance. I illustrate with one sparkling piece from among many, set in the larger description of the house of Rumor:

> Of werres, of pes, of mariages,
> Of reste, of labour, of viages,
> Of abood, of deeth, of lyf,
> Of love, of hate, acord, of stryf,
> Of loos, of lore, and of wynnynges,
> Of hele, of seknesse, of bildynges. . . .
> (1961–66)

Ten more anaphoric lines of the same kind of verbal enumeration follow; I need not quote them to demonstrate the point. This rhetorical flamboyance may well bring to mind the verbal wizardry of Humbert Humbert, but hardly the artless language of Defoe or the seemingly artless language of Henry James. If asked to explain what the *House of Fame* is about, Chaucer might well have responded as Nabokov did to a question about the meaning of *Lolita*—that it is about his love affair with the English language. Such a response may startle the reader intent on story, but it captures the intellectual dimension of rhetorical narrative by reminding us that beyond illusionary content is the real language of composition. Self-reflexive fiction, like Chaucer's and Nabokov's, directs us not only into illusion but out of it as well.

As a sequence of independent, self-defining structures, variously sized and shaped and more or less loosely linked together, the *House of Fame* violates what we are accustomed to regard as the aesthetic canons of the well-made fiction. But despite its structural discontinuity, its collage-like arrangement of individuated parts, the *House of Fame* is an irresistibly attractive poem. Its virtues lie close to the surface in the ubiquitous embodiments of authorial enthusiasm for verbal composition and design. The structural mode of segmental development, in its accent on primarily rhetorical values, is conducive to neither thematic continuity nor thematic depth. But since thematic interpretation has been prominent in studies of the *House of Fame,* I want to consider further that approach and try to demonstrate its limitations.

Because "fame" appears, in one way or another, in many of the parts of the poem, a degree of thematic continuity is undoubtedly present. Most interpretive commentary either seeks or assumes an underlying and pervasive linkage between Love and Fame, thereby resolving what J. A. W. Bennett has called "the initial surface-sense of confusion." [19] No doubt we can draw such connections, and no doubt medieval readers could too, as Bennett persuasively argues. But I think such reachings and delvings distract us from a textual surface, "confusing" though it may seem, that Chaucer fashioned as he did because he delighted in the resources of his vernacular language and its capacity to emulate the classics in elegance and range of expressiveness. Paul Ruggiers seeks to unify the poem through such a linking of Love, Fame, and Fortune. He argues that "the extravagant invention, the embellishment of glorious names, the energy and enthusiasm with which the poet rushes towards a conclusion would seem collectively to indicate his singleness of purpose." [20] "Singleness" of purpose seems to me a perverse interpretation of the features cited, an invention of the critic rather than a property of the poem.

To whatever degree we may wish to connect Love's tidings and Fame's dispositions, the question remains, to what depth

---

19. J. A. W. Bennett, *Chaucer's "Book of Fame"* (Oxford: Clarendon Press, 1968), p. xi.

20. Paul G. Ruggiers, "The Unity of Chaucer's *House of Fame,*" *Studies in Philology* 50 (1953): 25.

does the poem mine the subject of fame? Donald Howard approaches the truth in this observation about fame's "tidings": "The objective truth of a tiding is of no consequence; when it is reified in a tale or a poem or a book it becomes a *thing . . .* that exists in the world for a certain time." [21] Howard stresses the antiallegorical point that Chaucer's "universal rule of thumb was that everything is *exactly and only what it seems,* that every utterance is *exactly and only what it says.* The Pardoner is only the Pardoner; Chauntecleer, Chauntecleer . . . the Wife, the Wife." Howard pursues the ontological implication of this insight toward an ineffable "idea" in Chaucer's mind; I would develop it somewhat differently, however. Since the "objective truth of a tiding is of no consequence," being subject to ultimately unverifiable verbal redactions, the tiding itself mattered most to Chaucer, the verbal reification in tale or poem or book. I agree that the Wife is only the Wife. But the Wife is not the ultimate *thing* Howard insists on: ultimately the Wife is a verbal composition; there is no Wife. Nor is there a Dido, an Aeneas, or a talking eagle. There is only the written account, the poem, whose reality Chaucer was fully aware of and whose ironic relation to truth he recognized, puzzled over, and artfully explored.

In attempting to measure the poem's commitment to the theme of fame, we find only negative evidence through more than half of book 1. The subject is not broached until line 349, in Dido's lament for the loss of Aeneas and the shame his betrayal has brought to her name:

"O, wel-away that I was born!
For thorgh yow is my name lorn,
And alle myn actes red and songe
Over al thys lond, on every tonge.
O wikke Fame! for ther nys
Nothing so swift, lo, as she is!
O, soth ys, every thing ys wyst,
Though hit be kevered with the myst."
(345–52)

21. Howard, "Chaucer's Idea of an Idea," p. 49.

But how much does the poem make of the ontological possibilities of this passage? Let us consider the context. Sounding a passionate note of lament for lost reputation, these lines are a brief passage in a lengthy discourse on the subject of love betrayed. Both before this passage and after it the subject is not fame and reputation but betrayal, treated in a block of narrative that begins at line 255 with the story of Dido's love for Aeneas and his betrayal of her and ends at line 432 with Aeneas's departure for Italy. Just as fame is not developed as the theme of this segment, neither is betrayed love developed as the theme—or even *a* theme— that runs through the poem at large. It is the *telling* of this story of noble lovers—Howard's "reification"—that matters, a telling that in its intricacy and variety thoroughly overshadows the possible thematic implications of fame's tidings.

The telling moves in and out of the events it recounts. It begins with the cool distance of "Ther sawgh I grave how Eneas" (l. 253) and then, adopting a moralistic stance, introduces Chaucerian bathos into this high tale of love and death with a country proverb: "For, be Cryste, lo, thus yt fareth / 'Hyt is not al gold that glareth'" (ll. 271–72). The telling also at times reflects on itself:

Al this seye I be Eneas
And Dido . . .

. . . .
Therefore I wol seye a proverbe.
(286–89)

And of course the telling at another moment gives up its distance and dramatizes the forsaken Dido delivering her lamentation.

This segment's subject of betrayal is developed not in depth but *in extenso*, by *amplificatio*. The pathos of Dido's fate is abruptly dissolved into a bathetic transitional passage of narrative self-reflexiveness:

And al the maner how she deyde,
And alle the wordes that she seyde,
Whoso to knowe hit hath purpos,

Rede Virgile in Eneydos
Or the Epistle of Ovyde,
What that she wrot or that she dyde;
And nere hyt to long to endyte,
Be God, I wolde hyt here write.
                    (375–82)

When the event is thus distanced, the narrative proceeds to amplify the idea of betrayal in a flamboyant display of literary erudition. Over a span of thirty-eight lines we are treated to seven further examples from classical legend of women betrayed by men. Four of them are one-liners, plus a three-liner:

Eke lo! how fals and reccheles
Was to Breseyda Achilles,
And Paris to Oenone;
And Jason to Isiphile,
And eft Jason to Medea;
And Ercules to Dyanira,
For he left hir for Yole,
That made hym cache his deth, parde.
                    (397–404)

Framing this enumeration are the nine-line narrative of Demophon and Phyllis and the twenty-one-line narrative of Theseus and Ariadne. The differing lengths of treatment seem to be a matter of quantitative whim rather than qualitative significance. The effect is that of a glittering surface rather than meaningful depths. In fact meaning and thematic development are so thoroughly subordinated to surface effects and arbitrary elaborations that the "meaning" of this betrayal segment would not be significantly affected if Chaucer had used fewer or more supplementary exempla than the seven he chose. Nor would the meaning of either this section or the *House of Fame* as a whole have been significantly affected if the longest of the betrayal narratives had been, say, Paris and Oenone rather than Aeneas and Dido.

But we must recognize that betrayal itself is not the only subject of book 1, nor is it the only aspect of Chaucer's version of the Dido and Aeneas story. It is in the foreground only and arbitrarily as long as Chaucer chooses to attend to it. Also foregrounded is the subject of heroic mission and fateful destiny. This is the subject both before and after the love story: Aeneas chosen to fulfill a destiny determined by the gods, whose competing claims on him are also highlighted. His mother Venus vies with Juno, Jove's wife and a lifelong enemy of "al the Troianysshe blood," for Jove's favor in protecting Aeneas and preserving the Trojan nation. Then, too, we have a marvelously condensed and vivid version of the fall of Troy, and later, after the love adventure, we have the perilous voyage to Italy, also condensed and probably rendered more as Chaucer's tribute to the classical story and its distinguished redactions in "many a rowe / On Virgile or on Claudian, / Or Daunte" (ll. 448–50) than as an intrinsically relevant episode. The *House of Fame* is about all these subjects and many more, in addition to being about its own composition.

Faced with this situation—a poem about the Trojan War, about jealousies among the gods, about a protagonist who is both an amorous traitor and a heroic deliverer, about a woman's pain and suicide for love, about other stories of women betrayed in love, about the great classical tradition itself—critics would be prudent to rein in their interpretive impulses. To isolate one segment—any segment, such as Dido's exclamation about her reputation and fame—and invest it with special thematic significance seems misguided in the face of a poem demonstrably so expansive and varied in its interests and so unbiased in the treatment of its materials. The poem does not subordinate its materials to a controlling theme, in the manner of much Victorian and "traditional" fiction. The *House of Fame* is a brilliant mosaic, a literary entertainment, sanctioned by its classical—and in book 2 its "scientific"— erudition and rendered ceaselessly engaging by the narrative skills of its presentation. Chaucer's virtuosity is firmly based in the rhetorical devices of amplification (mainly varied repetition and digressive expansion) and abbreviation, as well as in the mastery of stylistic variation, from pathos to bathos, from the elevated to the ordinary, from eulogy to irony. The narrative proceeds in segments of irregular length, punctuated by shifts of perspective—sometimes subtle, sometimes abrupt—from the close-up of Dido's lament to the distanced viewpoints that objectify the content as painted images and, more distant still, as written sources.

Book 2 treats the subject of fame more extensively than does book 1 but not much more seriously. Again the point is not philosophical meaning so much as literary entertainment, which again is the product of Chaucer's rich verbal resources and extraordinary rhetorical skills. That the Eagle's discourse is a masterpiece of self-mocking *amplificatio* requires no detailed demonstration. Equally apparent are the abrupt disjunctions of style and perspective, from the cosmic distances and elevated language of the Eagle's discourse to the comic intimacy and plain talk of the captive Geffrey. Nor is continuity of plot any more in evidence than depth of theme. The Eagle promises to reveal in Fame's palace

> of Loves folk moo tydynges,
> . . . .
> And moo loves newe begonne,
> And longe yserved loves wonne,
> And moo loves casuelly
> That ben betyd. . . .
>
> (675–80)

But this is not at all what Geffrey finds there, though at the moment it makes an attractive expository utterance. This disjunctiveness and the priority of immediacy over any claims of continuity with past and future contribute to the collage-like character of the narrative. These features, combined with the Eagle's direct allusion to Geffrey's labors as a writer and Geffrey's own plea in the proem for Venus's help in his "telling," produce a predominantly "textual" poem. The overwhelming aesthetic impression is of a sparkling verbal surface, a surface that is not deeply charged with significance beyond or beneath itself.

Modern readers are newly discovering a capacity to delight in such "superficial" and "writerly" fictions without shame and without feeling the need to rationalize a "deeper meaning." Of course Borges, Calvino, Barth, and others did not invent the literature of delight. Annie Dillard's description of modernist (that is, experimental, or what I have called post-modernist) fiction and the values it expresses will sound familiar to those who have followed my account of the *House of Fame:*

> Technically as well as thematically it [modernist fiction] has taught us to admire the surfacing of structure and device. It prizes subtlety more than drama, concision more than expansion, parody more than earnestness, artfulness more than verisimilitude, intellection more than entertainment. It concerns itself less with social classes than with individuals, and, structurally, less with individual growth than with pattern of idea. It is not a statement but an artifact. Instead of social, moral, or religious piety or certainty, and emotional depth, it offers humor, irony, intellectual complexity, technical beauty, and a catalogue of the forms of unknowing.[22]

In summation Dillard points out that "the modernist direction in all the arts is a movement from what might be called the organic to the inorganic" (p. 63). Although the *House of Fame* prizes expansion as well as concision and concerns itself very little with either social classes or individuals, it otherwise answers to this characterization of a literature that has no designs on us—no ulterior meaning—other than its own design, its delight in artifice and the artful play with its own multivalent verbal materials. But Chaucer's modern readers have been loath to recognize the positive value of Matthew Arnold's negative judgment that denied Chaucer a place among the poets of "high seriousness." Resistance to that judgment, which often takes the form of "interpretation" that reveals a "serious" meaning behind an entertaining surface, is often misguided, particularly so, I think, in the case of the *House of Fame.* Glending Olson has recently demonstrated beyond doubt that medieval audiences were neither ashamed of literary pleasure nor unresponsive to it.[23] Though didactic literature was plentiful, all was not written for spiritual or moral doctrine, as Chaucer made equivocally clear at the close of the

22. Dillard, *Living by Fiction*, pp. 61–62.
23. Glending Olson, *Literature as Recreation in the Later Middle Ages* (Ithaca, N.Y.: Cornell Univ. Press, 1982).

Nun's Priest's Tale. Olson's amply documented thesis is that writers such as Boccaccio, Machaut, and Chaucer reaffirm "the stability and worth of such secular virtues as polite discourse, wit, and even recreational pleasure" (p. 200). Accordingly Olson offers the sound advice that "in regard to that type of literature which has no kernel, which exists solely 'causa delectandi,' it would seem that there is nothing to do but enjoy the sport" (p. 29).

Sport, I think, explains Chaucer's "man of gret auctorite," that puzzling absentee who has occasioned so much speculative interpretation. Donald Fry is right in asserting that the *House of Fame* "demonstrates metaphorically the unreliability of transmitted secular knowledge by satirizing the 'man of great authority' and authorities in general, breaking off as a deliberate fragment."[24] Those who would read the "man of gret auctorite" seriously, as a signification of Richard II or John of Gaunt or Boccaccio or Boethius, a man with an authoritative message to offer, must posit a literary structure more like Herbert's "The Collar" than the disjunct, improvisatory, multithematic poem before us. "The Collar" is a theme-centered poem, whose truth controls the meticulously ordered antitheses leading to climactic resolution in its concluding lines. Chaucer's poem, in contrast, states as one of its themes and illustrates throughout by its own example that there is no singular truth, only multiple perceptions. Because the aesthetic values of the *House of Fame* are expressed through segmentation and multiplicity, as I hope I have demonstrated, we can attribute to the old question of the "man of gret auctorite" a new meaninglessness.

Donald Fry qualifies the skepticism of the *House of Fame*

---

24. Donald K. Fry, "The Ending of the *House of Fame*," in *Chaucer at Albany*, ed. Rossell Hope Robbins (New York: Burt Franklin, 1975), p. 28. Similarly Patricia Kean has expressed in more general terms the idea that Chaucer could have had little more to say on the subject of Fame and Rumor, "and it would be unlike him . . . to end with any clearcut 'solution' to any of the problems he has raised" (*Chaucer and the Making of English Poetry* vol. 1 [London: Routledge and Kegan Paul, 1972], p. 111). See also Bennett, *Chaucer's "Book of Fame,"* p. 185.

with the important observation that the poem deals with the transmission of secular knowledge only. When Chaucer chose to look beyond the things of this world—including poetry and the writing of poetry—he did recognize a singular truth. As we shall consider in more detail in a later chapter, Chaucer's sense of a divine frame, toward whose fixity and stability the works of man might aspire, fundamentally qualified his poetics and differentiated his works from the rhetorical fictions of those twentieth-century confreres with whom he otherwise has so much in common.

Because the *House of Fame* offers so little objectified content, and therefore does not attract and absorb our interest in a depicted fiction of the world, of persons and actions in familiar settings, Delany is right enough in calling it an "intellectual exercise, though an extremely interesting exercise and an important one in the development of Chaucer's art."[25] In this sense all of the dream visions may be regarded largely as intellectual exercises, but it would be wrong to dismiss this approach to writing as exclusively a matter of genre. As the *House of Fame* itself illustrates, in all three of its main divisions—the narrative of Aeneas, the Eagle's discourse, and the personification allegory of Fame's court—Chaucer employs a variety of methods to accentuate his controlling presence. He does this not only by the self-parodic device of depicting the protagonist as a writer (or teller) out of control—appealing for help, digressing shamelessly, worrying about his accuracy—but also by rhetorical and structural means. The division of the work into parts of irregular size and shape; its asymmetrical and acentric structure; the abrupt shifts of style, mood, and even genre; and everywhere its manifest delight in the artifices of language—all of these characteristics are present in abundance in Chaucer's later and fictively richer works. Their presence dissociates Chaucer from the art of social or psychological realism and identifies him with that other great tradition of narrative fiction, of which he was the source and preeminent exemplar in English.

25. Delany, *Chaucer's "House of Fame,"* p. 68.

3

Rhetorical Composition

The *Book of the Duchess*

Compared with the *House of Fame*, the *Book of the Duchess* appears coherent and unproblematic. Its elegiac and consolatory purpose and, consistent with that, its predominantly courtly style would seem to disarm analysis and obviate interpretive debate. Of course such is not the case. Despite general agreement about the occasional nature of the poem, interpretation has nevertheless produced considerable controversy. Stylistic analysis has been suggestive at best and subordinated to thematic interpretation.[1] And rhetorical analysis of blocks of language, with its attendant emphasis on textuality, has scarcely been attempted. In this chapter I wish to set aside questions of interpretation (after making clear my reasons for doing so) and go on to demonstrate analytically what kind of poetic composition the *Book of the Duchess* is. Stylistic consistency and structural coherence are relative values, and analysis will show that however consistent and coherent the *Book of the Duchess* may appear to be, it is much closer to the disjunct and flamboyant *House of Fame* than to the nineteenth-century idea of the well-made, organically unified poem. Less overt than the *House of Fame* in its literary self-consciousness, the *Book of*

1. See the brief assessment by Robert O. Payne, *The Key of Remembrance: A Study of Chaucer's Poetics* (New Haven, Conn.: Yale Univ. Press, 1963), p. 125: "Books, experience, and vision are harmonized by stylistic insinuations which refer them all to a common and viable moral reality [viz. the 'lawe of kynde']." Payne alludes to "latent ironies" that suggest a tension against "the unity so nearly dominant in the poem" but quickly proceeds to consider their more overt manifestations in the *House of Fame*.

the Duchess nevertheless embodies the unspoken poetics that governs all of Chaucer's major poetic compositions.[2]

Like the *House of Fame*, but to a lesser extent, the *Book of the Duchess* has recently attracted interest as a poem about poetry. David Aers sees it as a poem that tests the efficacy of art as a consolation for personal grief, and he finds, contrary to prevailing opinion, that "art, rhetoric and language are finally consumed by the dreadful reality they have tried to control and make tolerable,"[3] that in fact the poem does not console. Traveling a similar route, Phillip Boardman partially defends the poem's consolatory effectiveness through a subtle interpretive strategy. He too sees the poem as a search for an efficacious poetic language; he stresses Chaucer's refusal to invoke the traditional consolation offered by Christianity and concludes that the *Book of the Duchess* is "a poem which has it both ways: it offers a celebration of the . . . lady and a commemoration of her relationship with the knight within a poem which suggests, nevertheless, that a poet . . . will not be able to offer words of comfort and solace."[4] This emphasis on the poem as a test of language—and the mainly negative result adduced by these critics—points to an important epistemological question that we shall pursue later on. From the narrower viewpoint of the present chapter, it appears that questions of the poem's textuality, its compositional structure and what we can infer from that about Chaucer's poetics, remain to be explored.

Two other studies illustrate the range of uncertainty that prevails in interpretive studies of the *Book of the Duchess*. Julia Ebel and Martin Stevens both attempt to place the poem in new contexts,[5] with the aim of freeing it, as Stevens puts it,

2. A similar point has been made by Diane M. Ross, "The Play of Genres in the *Book of the Duchess*," *Chaucer Review* 19 (1984): 1–13, who sees the poem as in part an *ars poetica*, a patchwork of genres, that fuses the poem's moral and aesthetic goals.

3. David R. Aers, "Chaucer's *Book of the Duchess*: An Art to Consume Art," *Durham University Journal* 69 (1977): 205.

4. Phillip C. Boardman, "Courtly Language and the Strategy of Consolation in the *Book of the Duchess*," *ELH* 44 (1977): 577–78.

5. Julia G. Ebel, "Chaucer's *The Book of the Duchess*: A Study in Medieval Iconography and Literary Structure," *College English* 29 (1967): 197–206;

from "standards of criticism which apply to the modern novel" and placing it in an aesthetic context more appropriate to a medieval poem. Thus, for example, he questions the widely held assumption that "character growth," especially in the dreamer-narrator, is an essential feature of the poem and maintains that "the Narrator-Dreamer fails to undergo any significant transformation."[6] Ebel moves further beyond the prevailing critical assumptions to seek aesthetic analogues in medieval visual art, from which she develops an interesting three-plane analysis of the poem, based on analogical principles of varied repetition and parallelism.[7] Unhappily, the hope that two such thoughtful commentaries would establish the basis for a new interpretive consensus is disappointed, for we are left to choose between mutually contradictory yet almost equally persuasive views of the poem. Both commentaries return to the old questions and respond to them in the old opposing ways:

1. Who is the protagonist, the focal point of the narrative? Stevens maintains that it is the Narrator-Dreamer, Ebel that it is the Black Knight.

2. Is the Narrator-Dreamer intelligent, compassionate, and tactful in his relationship with the Knight, or is he a dull, obtuse busybody? Stevens claims the former, Ebel the latter.

3. What is the theme of the poem? For Stevens it is Boethio-Christian consolation, conveyed through the simple profundity of the Narrator, whose life-affirming orientation Stevens feels is close to Chaucer's own. For Ebel

---

Martin Stevens, "Narrative Focus in *The Book of the Duchess:* A Critical Re-evaluation," *Annuale Mediaevale* 7 (1966): 16–32.

6. Stevens, "Narrative Focus," p. 19.

7. A comparable structural approach, though more concerned with philosophical implications, is pursued by Laurence Eldredge, "The Structure of *The Book of the Duchess,*" *Revue de l'Université d'Ottawa* 39 (1969): 133–51. See also Georgia Ronan Crampton, "Transitions and Meaning in *The Book of the Duchess,*" *JEGP* 62 (1963): 486–500; and Helen Philips, "Structure and Consolation in the *Book of the Duchess,*" *Chaucer Review* 16 (1981): 107–18. See also Ross, "The Play of Genres in the *Book of the Duchess.*"

> it is the "resonance" of grief as conveyed through the dignity of the Black Knight's diction of mourning, which the slow-witted and insensitive narrator can only partially and tardily understand.[8]

Though each view has much to recommend it, can both be right? Students of the poem have long been tempted simply to beg the real questions and answer yes, both are right and the greatness of the poem lies in its very capacity to contain, if not resolve, contradictions. But the poem deserves finer analysis, and if we find ourselves repeating contradictory answers to the old questions, perhaps it is because we have learned all we can from those questions. If my understanding of Ebel and Stevens is accurate, they are reaching toward an aesthetic analysis of the poem to complement or contrast with the psychological and dramatic interpretations we have in such abundance.

For medieval warrant to approach a medieval poem in this way—that is, as a formally composed or constructed entity— we need not look so far afield as iconography. As we have seen, medieval poets and rhetoricians understood composition in the literal sense of structuring poems with palpable verbal materials. I think structural analysis of the *Book of the Duchess* will support the view that Chaucer undertook the composition of the poem "as a man [who] has a house to build." He considered how he might best achieve "a skilful ordering of material," and then, "when due order [had] arranged the material in the hidden chamber of the mind, [he] let poetic art come forward to clothe the matter with words."[9] I use the language of the *Poetria nova* to stress the rhetorical character of poetic composition, but I should make clear that I

8. For a summary and bibliography of the debate over these issues, and citation to his own allegorical alternative, see D. W. Robertson, Jr., *"The Book of the Duchess,"* in *Companion to Chaucer Studies*, ed. Beryl Rowland, rev. ed. (New York: Oxford Univ. Press, 1979), pp. 403–13.

9. *Poetria nova*, trans. Margaret F. Nims (Toronto: Pontifical Institute of Medieval Studies, 1967), pp. 16–18. Chaucer paraphrases these formulations, to a different purpose, in *Troilus* 1 : 1065–69.

am concerned here primarily with the broad compositional sense of rhetoric, with the ways in which the poet chooses, shapes, and fits together his larger elements of narrative material. Perhaps the term *macro-rhetoric* indicates the difference of scale but sameness of kind in relation to the *micro-rhetoric* of ornaments and colors of style. The latter is indeed the principal concern of Geoffrey of Vinsauf in the sense that it constitutes by far the largest portion of the *Poetria nova*, and it elicits from him the same prescriptive treatment whereby in homology with the structure of the system of rhetoric as a whole, he defines, classifies, and exemplifies all the elements of discourse, from figures of speech down through phrases to individual words.

Chaucer's interest in thè vast array of ornaments in the many compartments of Geoffrey of Vinsauf's jewelry box has been a continuing concern of scholarly inquiry ever since Manly's provocative, if wrongly depreciatory, assessment.[10] Macro-rhetoric has aroused less interest among Chaucerian scholars,[11] perhaps because medieval rhetoricians like Geoffrey devoted less attention to it and offered fewer prescriptions and examples as guides for analysis. But Geoffrey's relative sparseness of treatment—confined to the first two hundred lines or so of the two-thousand-line *Poetria nova*—should not obscure for us the paramount importance of the principles he enunciated, principles that when properly applied, control the entire compositional structure.

10. See n. 20, chap. 1. For a summary, analysis, and bibliography of rhetorical criticism see Robert O. Payne, "Chaucer and the Art of Rhetoric," in Rowland, *Companion to Chaucer Studies,* pp. 38–57. See also Payne, *The Key of Remembrance,* and A. C. Spearing, *Criticism and Medieval Poetry,* 2d ed. (London: E. Arnold, 1972), pp. 51–75.

11. A notable exception is Dorothy Everett, "Some Reflections on Chaucer's 'Art Poetical,'" in her *Essays on Middle English Literature* (Oxford: Clarendon Press, 1955). The compositional structure of *Troilus* is discussed in Robert M. Jordan, *Chaucer and the Shape of Creation* (Cambridge: Harvard Univ. Press, 1967), pp. 75–95; also see William Provost, *The Structure of Chaucer's Troilus and Criseyde,* Anglistica 20 (Copenhagen: Rosenkilde og Bagger, 1974). Though not concerned with Chaucer, an invaluable contribution to the study of compositional rhetoric is Eugène Vinaver, *The Rise of Romance* (Oxford: Clarendon Press, 1971).

In his comprehensive study of the dream visions, Wolfgang Clemen speaks of Chaucer's "novel combinations of heterogeneous elements," especially in the early poetry.[12] Clemen has in mind not only sources of content—classical, Christian, Latin, French, Italian, English—but also stylistic elements, from high formal to low colloquial, and even generic types, the *Book of the Duchess* being an adaptation of the conventional medieval love vision to the purposes of classical elegy. Largely because of its elegiac character the *Book of the Duchess* is generally regarded as the most coherent of Chaucer's vision poems. Certainly in comparison with the *House of Fame*, as I suggested earlier, it gives the appearance of structural unity, and compared to the *Parlement of Foules* it seems a model of thematic clarity. Nevertheless, these comparisons are relative and limited, and we should not assume more coherence and unity than in fact exist. Within the particular coherence imparted by its elegiac purpose, the *Book of the Duchess* displays "combinations of heterogeneous elements" that are not only "novel" but remarkable for the aesthetic problems they present, and also for the structural solutions Chaucer employs.

As an elegy, the *Book of the Duchess* is both a eulogy of the dead and a consolation for those who remain to grieve. In comparison with some later examples of the genre, such as *Lycidas* and *Thyrsis*, the *Book of the Duchess* is extraordinarily indirect, even for a poetic form whose essence is artistic distance and refinement. As Clemen points out, it establishes its mode of indirectness at the very beginning as it employs a devious, roundabout approach to its thematic center via the Ceyx and Alcione story and other diversions (pp. 29–30). A major concern of commentary on the poem has indeed been whether some of the further reaches, both of subject matter and style, bear any relevance to the elegiac theme. Negative reports have been submitted by several investigators,[13]

---

12. Wolfgang Clemen, *Chaucer's Early Poetry*, trans. C. A. M. Sym (London: Methuen, 1963), p. 38.

13. Among these are Robert K. Root, *The Poetry of Chaucer*, rev. ed. (Boston: Houghton Mifflin, 1934); John S. P. Tatlock, *The Mind and Art of Chaucer* (Syracuse, N.Y.: Syracuse Univ. Press, 1950); Derek S. Brewer, *Chaucer* (London: Longmans, 1953).

whereas others have urged that even seeming irrelevancies play their subtle part in the total fabric of eulogy and consolation.[14] But none, I think, can deny the validity of Clemen's emphasis on indirection, postponement, and dilation as Chaucer's mode of progression through the course of the poem.

Whether Chaucer adhered consciously to Geoffrey of Vinsauf's structural advice we can never know, though we can doubt. Nevertheless, the poem appears to dispose itself into clearly defined sections, most of which display discernible structural outlines and follow orderly principles of internal organization. Individually these parts exemplify several forms of *amplificatio*, for example the knight's account of his first approach to his lady (ll. 1190–1245), the description of the lady "White" (ll. 805–1035), the narrative of the journey to Morpheus's cave (ll. 153–91), which is itself a part of the larger intercalated narrative of Ceyx and Alcione (ll. 62–220). The aggregate of these parts and many others comprises an irregular mixture of lyric and narrative elements, plus the problematic "drama" of the narrator-dreamer's role. The primary aesthetic effect of this aggregation, it seems to me, is variety: a richness and diversity of materials that Chaucer has amplified to the outer limits of order and containment. Clemen's passing comparison to the exuberance and flamboyance of the later Gothic style in architecture seems apt indeed. From this point of view the task of criticism is to discover and articulate an idea of composition, a poetics, that renders such a multiplicity of materials aesthetically understandable.

Compositional analysis of the poem will make clear that the controlling compositional idea is expository, in the sense that the aim is aggregation and display rather than development. Meaning, accordingly, tends to become multiple rather than unitary, and as a consequence narrative continuity, dramatic consistency, and organic unity diminish in relevance.

14. Among these are George Lyman Kittredge, *Chaucer and His Poetry* (Cambridge: Harvard Univ. Press, 1915); Bertrand H. Bronson, "*The Book of the Duchess* Re-opened," *PMLA* 67 (1952): 863–81; John Lawlor, "The Pattern of Consolation in *The Book of the Duchess*," *Speculum* 31 (1956): 626–48; John Gardner, "Style as Meaning in the *Book of the Duchess*," *Language and Style* 2 (1969): 143–71.

Thus the relation between, say, the knight's overheard love plaint early in the poem and his detailed, circumstantial account of his courtship and marriage near the end becomes one of parallelism between similar but separate and separated statements.[15] Similarly, as we shall see, the interlocutory functions of the dreamer, instead of cohering in a unified sensibility, are shaped by the separate contexts in which they occur and remain incompletely resolved, leaving gaps in the characterization of the dreamer.

The clear articulation of structural parts implicit in Geoffrey of Vinsauf's metaphor of the poetic "house" is readily demonstrable in the *Book of the Duchess*. Such accentuated textuality reflects a poetics that prizes verbal craftsmanship and clearly differentiates medium from story. Chaucer's regular use of verbal formulas at the opening and closing of major sections is the most natural and obvious means of articulation. Between smaller compositional units and parts of parts, where less flamboyant means of articulation are required, Chaucer generally employs the method of abrupt, unadorned juxtaposition. The outline below is intended to identify elements of composition and structural emphases and to assess the relations of parts to one another and to the whole. My division of the poem into eleven principal sections, irregular in size and shape, is arbitrary to some extent. Some sections could be enlarged and others further subdivided, and my subsequent discussion will recognize that some are closely related substantively as well as structurally, whereas others are distinctly separated. But I think the outline reflects the compositional facts, and my titles and subtitles define sections that are structurally individuated and reasonably self-consistent.

1. Lines 1–61   Introduction. The poet-narrator-
                           dreamer's insomnia and his reading
2. Lines 62–217   Tale of Ceyx and Alcione

---

15. On the juxtaposition of parallel episodes in the service of the theme of "acceptance of mortality" see Helen Philips, "Structure and Consolation in the *Book of the Duchess*."

		122–217	Alcione's dream
			132–91	Juno's messenger to the cave of Morpheus
			192–211	Alcione's vision of Ceyx
			212–217	Conclusion of dream and tale
3.	Lines 218–90	Narrator's explicit transition back to his "first matere"	
		218–69	His obtuse gloss of Ceyx and Alcione tale
		270–90	The end of his insomnia
4.	Lines 291–343	Dream begins. Description of dreamer's surroundings	
		291–320	Auditory
		321–43	Visual
5.	Lines 344–443	The hunt. Description: conventional garden imagery	
6.	Lines 444–559	Description of black knight	
		475–86	Knight's love-plaint (overheard by dreamer)
		487–559	Transitional dialogue. Further description of knight
7.	Lines 560–709	Knight's explanation of his sorrow (addressed directly to dreamer)	
		560–616	Series of rhetorical figures of love service
		617–86	Chess game with Fortune
		687–709	Personal lamentation
8.	Lines 710–57	Transitional dialogue (comic)	
9.	Lines 758–1311	Knight's second explanation (sequential account of his love service)	

	760–804	Dedication of himself to Love	
	805–1143	First sight of lady	
		817–1040	Eulogy of lady
			817–984 Physical qualities
			985–1040 Moral qualities
		1041–1143	Transitional dialogue
			1054–1087 Digression (erudite catalogue)
	1144–1220	Beginning of love for lady, in secret	
	1221–35	First supplication to lady (denied)	
	1257–97	Second supplication (accepted)	
	1298–1311	Dialogue: conclusion of knight's account, and completion of dreamer's understanding	
10.	Lines 1311–24	Conclusion of dream	
11.	Lines 1325–34	Conclusion of poem	

Acknowledging the diversity of elements and styles and narrative foci that constitute the composition, we nonetheless recognize readily that the heart of the poem as an elegy lies in sections 5–9. We shall concentrate our attention there. To point out that a sequence of some one thousand lines constitutes the heart of a thirteen-hundred-line poem might seem only minimally helpful, but the ordering principles of that heterogeneous, prolix, and devious sequence are far from self-evident. Analysis of the central structure will help us to distinguish clearly between principal and secondary features and finally to reach a better understanding of the aesthetic character of the whole poem. We shall look first, then, at sections 5 through 9 and reserve comment on earlier matter, notably the Ceyx and Alcione story, until later.

Section 5, where the dream hunt begins, presents the atmosphere of garden, forest, and meadow in which love flourishes, as everyone knows who is familiar with the conventions of the French love vision.[16] Each tall, strong, beautiful, leafy tree stands ten or twelve feet from its neighbors, forming a shaded, temperate paradise thick with flowers to rival the stars of heaven and inhabited by more lovely harts, hinds, and other benevolent creatures than Argus himself could reckon. Commentators have noted appreciatively the Chaucerian touches of this essentially conventional passage, such as the dreamer's exit with a horse from his bedchamber, and the colloquial conversation in which he learns that the proprietor of the hunt is the emperor Octavian. These touches, mainly concerning the dreamer, are indeed engaging, and in their humor and their slight incongruity with the courtly context they adumbrate some of the central interpretive problems of the poem. What we note here about the dreamer's role is largely true elsewhere as well. It possesses an interest of its own that is distinct from love doctrine and from elegy, and at the same time it serves a compositional function as a transitional link between parts of the poetic structure. Both stylistically and substantively it is separate from the matter of love, though related to it. The mode of that relationship and the extent to which the poem accommodates these distinct levels of

16. For a comprehensive summary of conventional elements in French love visions, including the "hunt of love," see James I. Wimsatt, *Chaucer and the French Love Poets: The Literary Background of the "Book of the Duchess"* (Chapel Hill: Univ. of North Carolina Press, 1968). A convenient gathering of Chaucer's French sources is Barry A. Windeatt, ed. and trans., *Chaucer's Dream Poetry: Sources and Analogues*, Chaucer Studies 7 (Cambridge, England: D. S. Brewer, 1982).

interest will continue to concern us. But the dominant effect of section 5 is to establish the richly connotative setting within which we encounter the knight in black.

Section 6 consists essentially of description of the knight, though it also contains the knight's brief but formally distinct, important, and highly problematic love plaint, which I shall consider separately. In section 6 more than one hundred lines describe the handsome, noble mien of this young man; his debonair, courteous, and genteel bearing; and, above all and at length, his immersion in grief. Given the likelihood of an allegorical correspondence with John of Gaunt, the primary force of these passages is nonetheless to eulogize the qualities of "cortesie" as personified in this noble and humane figure, who so perfectly fulfills the expectations fixed by the poetic setting. We should bear in mind, as Clemen reminds us, that "the aim of French love-visions was predominantly didactic," [17] and although Chaucer loosened the rigid methods of his predecessors, such as set dialogues of instruction in love doctrine between personified abstractions, the celebration of courtly values remains a major concern of the *Book of the Duchess*. The eulogistic presentation of the knight in section 6 is the first of a series of direct contributions to this undertaking, following the more figurative, indirect tribute effected through the language and imagery of the hunt in section 5. In addition to the dreamer's third-person description, the knight's own language perfectly reflects the qualities of courtly grace and magnanimity, and this despite the heavy burden of his personal sorrow. These qualities of the knight are highlighted against the colloquial language and respectful manner of the dreamer. Though here as elsewhere the dreamer is a more interesting figure in his own right than the narrating figures in the French love visions, our sense of the representational and dramatic quality of the role should be tempered by an awareness of its structural function. Disarmingly "natural" as the representation is, the primary function of the role in its compositional context is to effect a transition from one form of

17. Clemen, *Chaucer's Early Poetry*, p. 25.

courtly exposition to another, that is, from the extensive third-person description of the knight in section 6 to a different courtly material, which will be presented in the knight's own words in section 8. The transition is made explicit in the words of the dreamer:

> And telleth me of your sorwes smerte;
> Paraunter hyt may ese youre herte,
> That semeth ful sek under your syde.
>
> (555–57)

Thus section 6 is closed and section 7 introduced. Before turning to section 7, we shall look at the brief love plaint imbedded in the otherwise essentially descriptive section 6.

Interpretation of this brief lyric (ll 475–86) has always been a contentious matter. Some hold that having overheard this plaint the dreamer must have realized from the start that the knight was in mourning for his dead lady. From this assumption arises the conception of the tactful dreamer consoling the mourner by patiently encouraging him to release his grief, up to the final point of personal catharsis at the end of the dream.[18] Others hold that the dreamer is too obtuse to understand the meaning of this poetic expression of sorrow and that he better serves Chaucer's purpose in the character of a naive but good-hearted interrogator.[19] A further interpretation holds that the language of the plaint is hyperbolic in the conventional manner of the *complainte d'amour* and not to be understood by the dreamer (or audience) as referring to the death of a specific lady.[20] While Clemen follows the views of Kittredge and Bronson and maintains that it is "out of the question for us to think of him [the dreamer] as naive, obtuse, or unintelligent" (p. 50),

18. In addition to Clemen, advocates of this view include Kittredge, Bronson, and Lawlor, all cited in n. 14 above, and James R. Kreuzer, "The Dreamer in *The Book of the Duchess*," *PMLA* 66 (1951): 543–47.

19. Advocates of this view include Kemp Malone, *Chapters on Chaucer* (Baltimore: Johns Hopkins Univ. Press, 1951); Donald C. Baker, "The Dreamer Again in *The Book of the Duchess*," *PMLA* 70 (1955): 279–82; Stephen Manning, "That Dreamer Once More," *PMLA* 71 (1956): 540–41.

20. W. H. French, "The Man in Black's Lyric," *JEGP* 56 (1957): 231–41. See also Baker, "The Dreamer Again."

he also reminds us, as have Baker, French, and others, that the knight's speeches, including the overheard plaint, contain many of the terms of conventional lament. We would therefore have to allow for the opposing possibility that the uncourtly dreamer might indeed have "misunderstood" the import of the plaint. Thus stated in terms of the dreamer's understanding or misunderstanding, the issue seems not to admit of clear resolution. However, if we remind ourselves of the poem's primary concern with lament, elegy, and consolation, the question of the dreamer's psychic consistency becomes secondary. In other words, the interpretive problem seems more tractable to compositional than to dramatic solutions. The context in section 6 of eulogistic courtly description of the grieving knight and the extensive presentation of him as a man of gentle speech and manners far outweigh in impact and thematic relevance the brief passages depicting the dreamer's responses. The dreamer's response is encouraging:

> But, sir, oo thyng wol ye here?
> Me thynketh in gret sorowe I yow see.
> But certes, sire, yif that yee
> Wolde ought discure me youre woo,
> I wolde, as wys God helpe me soo,
> Amende hyt, yif I kan or may.
>
> (546–51)

But by the time he responds some sixty lines have elapsed since the eleven-line plaint. The context of the dreamer's words is the large presentation of the man in black. The poem would thus seem not to display a continuity that warrants our regarding these words of the dreamer as primarily a logical or a dramatic response—whether tactful or stupid—to the earlier "disclosure." On the contrary, in the disjunct, discontinuous narrative mode of the poem, the dreamer's transitional function overrides his dramatic function and characterization. Serving primarily as the agent of movement from one element of the poem's matter to another, the dreamer takes on the traits requisite at a given stage of the poem's progress. This is not to deny that Chaucer has endowed the dreamer with certain consistently recognizable personality traits but to question the basis for regarding the dreamer as a unified consciousness, developing consistently through experience. In the present instance what the dreamer knows or does not know seems less important than the need for the poem to move. The knight's *complainte d'amour* is one means of amplifying the presentation of sorrow and lament, and the dreamer's later words constitute less a personal response to it than a dramatized transition to new matter.

In compositional terms the knight's lyric illustrates well Chaucer's peculiarly original eclecticism in which, as Clemen has shown, he combines elements of lament, elegy, and *complainte* in the service of his larger purpose of elegiac consolation. If this integration of materials is not as complete as we might wish, if the effect is not psychologically coherent and fully plausible, we should recognize that within the limits of his compositional style Chaucer has achieved a remarkably effective mixture of materials, though not an organic unity. The expanded, "humanized" role of the dreamer indeed illustrates Chaucer's movement toward a new structural naturalism, but "characterization," especially psychological coherence, remains a secondary feature of the role. Primarily the role serves to close the seams of the poem's fabric, to maintain a narrative momentum (however dilatory), and to negotiate some awkward leaps of continuity.

In sum, section 6 presents a striking variety of materials related to the knight, most of it in the dreamer-narrator's third-person description but some of it in the knight's own words, including both those heard and those overheard by the dreamer. If the dreamer does not understand what he overhears as a reference to a specific death, it may well be that Chaucer intended no such denotation at this stage of his poem. From a general, eclectically conventional presentation of the context of personal loss, he will move slowly into a more circumstantial presentation. The words of the dreamer (ll. 546–51), quoted above, prepare the way.

In section 7 the black knight, following the dreamer's show of friendly concern, undertakes to explain to him the cause of

his sorrow. As an amplification of the compressed and gener-
alized *complainte d'amour* overheard earlier by the dreamer,
section 7 expands the highly charged rhetoric of courtly lyric
and conventional lament into a freer poetic form. The language is still figurative and the sentiment highly idealized,
and therefore its value as an "explanation" of the knight's condition is qualified, especially from the literalist viewpoint articulated here by the dreamer. Section 7 falls into three parts.
The first is mainly a series of extravagant figures of love pain,
largely borrowed from the conventions of classical lament and
French and Petrarchan love poetry. For example:

> "This ys my peyne wythoute red,
> Alway deynge and be not ded,
>
> . . . .
> . . . y am sorwe, and sorwe ys y.
>
> . . . .
> Myn hele ys turned into seknesse,
> In drede ys al my sykernesse;
> To derke ys turned al my lyght,
> My wyt ys foly, my day ys nyght."
> (587–610)

The second part of section 7 is the chess game with Fortune,
in which that "trayteresse fals" took from the hapless knight
his "fers." This metaphorical narrative, elaborated to the extent of a small allegory, ends on a high poetic level as the
knight cries out in despair, " . . . through that draughte I
have lorn / My blysse; allas! that I was born!" (ll. 685–86). In
the third part, shorter than the other two, the knight follows
the account of the chess game with a personal lament, concluding section 7 with a classical allusion in the high style:

> "Allas! than am I overcome!
> For that ys doon ys not to come.
> I have more sorowe than Tantale."
> (707–9)

As a whole, section 7, in the fullest rhetorical sense of *amplificatio*, is a lavish enlargement, in varied forms, of the earlier
complainte d'amour and its stylized context of courtly descrip-

tion of the knight. We need say little more about it here except to note a line that has caused much difficulty in connection with the problem, considered earlier, of the dreamer's "failure to understand."

When the knight exclaims,

> "Y wreche, that deth hath mad al naked
> Of al the blysse that ever was maked,"
>
> (577–78)

should not the dreamer, and we too, recognize at once that the speaker is lamenting the death of his lady? Such a literal interpretation cannot be ruled out, but the highly allusive context tends to resolve the issue in favor of metaphorical interpretation. The knight goes on to compare himself to Sisyphus and complain that his fate is to be "Alwey deynge and be not ded" (588), which we recognize as an idealization of sorrow—profoundly serious, but an idealization. The dreamer's response, however, is different from ours. It doesn't occur for some 150 lines, in the passage that I have designated section 8, which we shall consider in a moment. Meanwhile the chess-game passage occurs, followed by the knight's personal lamentation (ll. 687–709). Thus concludes section 7, an exposition, in three extensively amplified parts, of the knight's emotional state: the stylized antitheses of love pain, the attenuated figure of the chess game with Fortune, and the personal lamentation.

The return of the dreamer effects a change both in tone and in matter. In this brief transitional section 8, the dreamer responds compassionately but oddly inappropriately to the knight's long speech. His response consists mainly of an erudite catalogue of classical tragedies (ll. 722–40), which he finally misapplies when he contrasts these instances of real grief with the knight's lamentation over the loss of a mere chess piece:

> But ther is no man alyve her
> Wolde for a fers make this woo!
>
> (740–41)

We find the dreamer's incredulity more than a little comical. The ironic humor arises from the contrast between the dreamer's earnest literal-mindedness and our own understanding of the metaphorical dimension of the knight's language. As in most problems of Chaucerian interpretation, we do not choose between extremes of literalness: if the knight's subject is not really a lost "fers," neither is it plainly understandable, at this stage of the poem, as a dead lady. The superiority of our understanding of the chess metaphor to the understanding embodied in the dreamer's response is based in the gentility we share with the knight, a gentility—measured by language—from which the dreamer is excluded. This essential point is obscured if we insist too strongly on knowing literally whom the "fers" represents and whether the dreamer knows. At this stage the poem is still concerned with the amplification of grief in highly figurative courtly language. In section 8 the dreamer is moving the poem to another stage, in which the knight will abandon the figurative forms of lyric and allegorical complaint for an essentially narrative account of his love service: courtship, marriage, and finally the death of his wife.

As in many another transitional passage, in the *Book of the Duchess* and elsewhere, Chaucer does not resist the errant impulse to endow the narrator with signs of a life of his own, regardless of the delays and diversions in narrative continuity that result. But as we saw earlier, the signs of life do not easily cohere into a consistent characterization. Here too (ll. 710–57) the function of the dreamer-narrator's role is multiple rather than unitary. The several ways in which the role works are by no means entirely consistent with one another or with a monothematic conception of the poem. While the dreamer's insistently literal interpretation of the chess-game allegory disengages him temporarily from the serious purposes of elegy and indeed arouses antithetical responses of comedy, nevertheless his speech is in a different and subtler way germane to the issue. His list of classical exempla, though misapplied by him, conveys relevant and touching reverberations to his audience, including, presumably, John of Gaunt as well as ourselves. The stories of Medea, Dido, Phyllis, Echo, Samson—legendary exemplars of suffering and unnatural death—remind us all that pain, grief, and inexplicable loss are part of the human condition. The extent to which this material "characterizes" the dreamer is highly dubious, not the least of the doubts arising from the fact, as we shall see, that some three hundred lines later a closely similar catalogue of classical exempla, similarly half-humorous in its context, emits from the mouth of the knight. This flamboyant erudition—we noted in the *House of Fame* a similar catalogue of classical exempla that served less to characterize the speaker than to display the author in full verbal flight—is a further instance of Chaucer's interest in the crafting of artful surfaces.[21] The aesthetic principle holding such parts of the poem together is one of accommodation, and we are probably unfaithful to the text and the spirit of the poem if we press too hard toward a concept of integration, whether of organic characterization or unified theme.

Thus the narrative moves unevenly through section 8, diverting us to momentary absorption in the charms and vagaries of our guide but leading finally into the knight's large-scale, final exposition of the source and nature of his sorrow. The verbal cue is explicitly rendered with the dreamer's urgent request and the knight's willing compliance:

> "Good sir, telle me al hooly
> In what wyse, how, why, and wherfore
> That ye have thus youre blysse lore."
> "Blythely," quod he; "com sytte adoun!
> I telle the upon a condicioun
> That thou shalt hooly, with al thy wyt,
> Doo thyn entent to herkene hit."
>
> (746–52)

---

21. Aers, "Chaucer's *Book of the Duchess*," sees these passages as "ironic dismissal of . . . moral didacticism" working through the "flat, mindless accumulation of *exempla* and through the irrelevance of the examples to the knight's case" (p. 204).

Plainly we are to hear a patient and detailed account, additional to what we have already absorbed. For this version indirection and figurative means are to be abandoned in favor of a circumstantial narrative of the course of the knight's love service, circumstantial, that is, within the non-naturalistic limits of courtly discourse.

The knight's sequential narrative of his love service forms by far the largest part of the poem. My outline is perhaps sufficient to denote the substance of this section and to indicate the comparative coherence that endows it with structural identity. The step-by-step account of the knight's courtship, detailing his anguish and his hope, provides space for dilatory intercalations, and we have the delicately rendered eulogy of the lady White (ll. 817–1033), itself a sequence of clearly articulated parts. In filling out this lengthy section of the poem, Chaucer employs the conventional courtly attitudes and stylized formulas; through sympathy and poetic skill he imparts to them a compelling seriousness and enduring interest.

But for all its courtly consistency, section 9 is not without its imbalances and internal clashes. As we have come to expect, the dreamer is at least the partial source of these irregularities. The one-hundred-line passage of transitional dialogue (ll. 1041–1143) connecting the eulogy of the lady White with the beginning of the knight's account of his secret love for her, serves not only to move the narrative along in typically explicit fashion but also to disturb, if not shatter, the prevailing atmosphere of elegy and courtly diffidence. One can sympathize with the judgment of Derek Brewer and others that in such instances the "immature" poet simply lost control of his material.[22] But when tested against the poet's general practice,

---

22. In *Chaucer* Derek S. Brewer speaks of the "lack of poetic control" in *Book of the Duchess,* especially evidenced in the humorous passages, which Chaucer "certainly could *not* have intended, as can be seen from the circumstances and intention of the poem" (p. 47). Similar views are expressed by Root, *The Poetry of Chaucer,* pp. 59–63, and Tatlock, *The Mind and Art of Chaucer,* p. 30. On the other hand, see Malone: "Chaucer introduces a comic ele-

normative judgments that emerge from hypotheses of generic purity and poetic intention, prove invalid or at best misleading. The effect of the questionable passage in section 9 depends on recognition of its digressive character, which in turn is underscored by its length. Therefore, to illustrate the effect, rather lengthy quotation is required here. Having delivered his extensive eulogy of his lady, the knight, prodded by the dreamer's sympathetic but to him inadequate responses, undertakes a further asseveration of the depth of his love and dedication:

> "I wolde thoo
> Have loved best my lady free,
> Thogh I had had all the beaute
> That ever had Alcipyades,
> And al the strengthe of Ercules,
> And therto had the worthynesse
> Of Alysaunder, and al the rychesse
> That ever was in Babyloyne,
> In Cartage, or in Macedoyne
> Or in Rome, or in Nynyve;
> And therto also hardy be
> As was Ector, so have I joye,
> That Achilles slough at Troye—
> And therfore was he slayn alsoo
> In a temple, for bothe twoo
> Were slayne, he and Antylegyus,
> And so seyth Dares Frygius,
> For love of Polixena—
> Or ben as wis as Mynerva,
> I wolde ever, withoute drede,
> Have loved hir, for I moste nede."
>
> (1054–74)

In itself the extravagance of classical allusions supports properly enough the emotional point the knight is striving to enforce. It does so in the fashion of rhetorical *amplificatio* and in disregard of the cost to narrative progress and continuity. But

---

ment into the very heart of his elegy, and this without spoiling the elegiac effect, a piece of technical virtuosity beyond praise" (*Chapters on Chaucer*, p. 39). Further to the question of the poet's "immaturity," see n. 28 below.

what of the story of Hector, Achilles, Antilochus, and Polyx-ena—attributed to Dares Phrygius? Masterfully compressed though this narrative is, its inclusion here seems indeed a gra-tuitous, half-comic digression. These are not the words of the dreamer of dubious taste and refinement, who uttered a simi-lar and similarly ill-applied catalogue of erudition some three hundred lines earlier, as we noted above. In both cases Chau-cer appears willing to introduce passages of some length that seem to disrupt both generic and thematic consistency as well as the tone and atmosphere of elegy. Another casualty is con-sistency of characterization, since similar erudite digressions are assigned to the courtly knight and the common dreamer-narrator. The attribution of such passages to the poet's imma-turity loses much of its force when we note that similar pas-sages abound in even his most mature work.[23] Of course we can continue to regard such passages as imperfections, but in doing so we would be presupposing aesthetic criteria—such as tightness of structure and economy of means—that appar-ently exerted little influence on medieval poets, if our analysis of Chaucer's work is any guide.

As enunciated by Geoffrey of Vinsauf, the first principle of *amplificatio* is as follows:

> Although the meaning is one, let it not come content with one set of apparel. Let it vary its robes and assume different rai-ment. Let it take up again in other words what has already been said; let it reiterate, in a number of clauses, a single thought. Let one and the same thing be concealed under mul-tiple forms—be varied and yet the same.[24]

As though to comply with this rule, Chaucer's narrator directs the courtly exposition to its final iteration:

---

23. See, for example, my discussion of *Troilus* in *Chaucer and the Shape of Creation*, pp. 75–95. That inconsistencies of this kind are an essential element of Chaucer's style is Charles Muscatine's thesis in *"The Canterbury Tales: Style of the Man and Style of the Work,"* in *Chaucer and Chaucerians*, ed. Derek S. Brewer (University, Ala.: Univ. of Alabama Press, 1966).

24. Geoffrey of Vinsauf, *Poetria nova*, p. 24.

"Now, goode syre," quod I thoo,
"Ye han wel told me herebefore,
Hyt ys no nede to reherse it more,
How ye sawe hir first, and where.
But wolde ye tel me the manere
To hire which was your firste speche,
Therof I wolde yow beseche;
And how she knewe first your thoght,
Whether ye loved hir or noght.
And telleth me eke what ye have lore,
I herde yow telle herebefore."

(1126–36)

The knight obliges, and the next 150 lines—except for a few diversions of the kind we have noted—recount in loving and sequential detail the stages of the knight's courtship, marriage, and finally, in unequivocal, unmetaphorical terms, his loss: "She ys ded!"[25] With this ultimate clarification, gratuitous or not, the consolatory and literary aims of the poem are fulfilled, though the poem is not quite over. Some formal considerations remain to be attended to: section 10 succinctly closes the dream frame, and section 11 concludes the poem, returning to the literary note on which it began, the dreamer waking to "put this sweven in ryme."

The view I have taken is essentially synchronic, seeing the poem's many structural irregularities and violations of tone and scale as possibilities, if not requirements, inherent in a compositional mode that works in blocks of language, its many versions of courtly eulogy and consolation stitched together by transitional passages often incongruent in tone and of dubious thematic relevance. There is of course a diachronic, or temporal, developmental, dimension to the poem. That is the dimension regarded by Clemen and others when they emphasize the indirectness and "suspense" that delay the final

25. Aers, "Chaucer's *Book of the Duchess*," regards "She ys ded" as the dreadful reality that art, rhetoric, and language have tried and failed to make tolerable (p. 205). A similar view is expressed by Boardman, "Courtly Language and the Strategy of Consolation," p. 574.

"She ys ded!" The diachronic emphasis has attributed most of this deviousness of narration to the mind and personality of the dreamer-narrator, a figure who as a result has grown in psychic stature far beyond the ancillary role he plays in the poem. Without denying the sparks of vitality that fly from him, I have tried to show how in Chaucer's hands he serves the rhetorical purpose of disposing the parts of a richly varied poetic exposition. I have viewed the central matter of the poem (ll. 344–1310) as an array of poetic forms—lyric, narrative, descriptive, didactic, and to an extent dramatic—in the service of a noble ethic and a compassionate purpose. The dilatory, spasmodic movement of the poem is consistent with the techniques of *amplificatio* and affords the scope and aesthetic context for Chaucer's emotional range and poetic virtuosity.

If the compositional principles I have adduced from this analysis of the central matter of the poem are valid, they should simplify discussion of that controversial excrescence, the Ceyx and Alcione story. Like many less prominent passages we have considered, this too has attracted both praise for its subtlety and blame for its immaturity. The controversy is more satisfactorily defined—though probably not fully resolved—from a structural standpoint. Plainly the narrative forms a self-contained rhetorical unit beginning "This was the tale" (l. 61) and ending "I have told this thyng / Of Alcione and Seys the kyng" (ll. 219–20). From a thematic point of view Chaucer's purpose in inserting this tale can be justified and its "fundamentally vital relation to the dream-content," though "subtle and disguised," can be explained in Clemen's terms: "Just as Halcyone was comforted by the reappearance of her husband in a dream, the knight was comforted by recalling his dead wife to mind as he told his own story." [26] If we accept this interpretation of the general thematic relevance of the tale, we still face some troublesome incongruities, one of them the narrator's own explanation for telling the tale: at considerable length he relates it only to his personal problem of

---

26. Clemen, *Chaucer's Early Poetry*, p. 31.

insomnia (ll. 221–69). If this humorous mis-glossing does not diminish our appreciation of the tale's subtler relevance, neither can we easily dismiss it as an artistic blemish or "immaturity." Humor is not the exclusive prerogative of children and beginners, nor is Chaucer's maturest work free of this mixture of effects, as I suggested earlier.

But the tale itself provides further inconsistencies of this kind. As my outline indicates, the visit of Juno's messenger to the cave of Morpheus constitutes a substantial segment of the tale. This humorous and thoroughly engrossing episode—Muscatine calls it "a moment of intense, comic practicality in the midst of conventionalism"[27]—carries us a long way from the thematic concern with grief and consolation, however subtly conceived. Yet surely it does not spoil the poem. We are perfectly willing, even delighted, to accept it as part of a tale that elsewhere conveys delicate and compassionate overtones. And we accept the tale itself in similar spirit, as part of a poem not consistently of a piece, though true enough to its own aesthetic principles. The poem's rhetorical orientation and inorganic structure can accommodate this independently wrought and engagingly told tale, just as the tale can accommodate the attenuated, humorous, yet masterfully controlled account of the journey to Morpheus.[28]

Perhaps we can say in summation that if the *Book of the Duchess* lacks the smoothly integrated texture of an organic unity, it amply compensates with its aggregative brilliance, its rhetorical energy, and its rich variety of tone and nuance. Although not as overtly self-reflexive as the *House of Fame* and

27. Charles Muscatine, *Chaucer and the French Tradition* (Berkeley: Univ. of California Press, 1960), p. 105.

28. This episode illustrates nicely an aspect of Chaucer's artistic control not widely appreciated. His versification displays a mastery of speech rhythms unexcelled in English except perhaps by Pope. The crisp rhythms of the eager messenger's arrival—"This messenger com fleynge faste / And cried, 'O, Ho! awake anoon!'"—contrast beautifully with the attenuated, somnolent rhythm of Morpheus's response: "This god of slep with hys oon ye / Cast up, axed, 'Who clepeth ther?'" We might say that at this early stage of his poetic career Chaucer was untried, but hardly immature or out of control.

the other dream visions, the *Book of the Duchess* clearly associates itself with the tradition of artful discourse—at the beginning with

> fables
> That clerkes had in olde tyme,
> And other poets, put in rime
> (52–54)

and at the end with the speaker's mock-modest asseveration,

> That I wol, be processe of tyme,
> Fonde to put this sweven in ryme
> As I can best.
> (1331–33)

But regardless of how little the poem *says* about writing, what
it *does* is display a verbal artistry; an elegance, wit, and refinement; a joy in the play of language rare in any age and beyond
praise in a young poet writing in the artistic dawn of vernacular English. In the face of Chaucer's accomplishment, we
must reverse the emphasis of Robinson's patronizing judgment: "What is most remarkable, the poem, in spite of the artificial tradition to which it belongs, expresses real feeling." [29]
The notion of an antipathy between feeling and artifice does
not apply to Chaucer. For him the artificial tradition was not a
hindrance but a vital framework, providing materials and direction for his innovative artistry in the English vernacular.

29. F. N. Robinson, ed., *The Works of Geoffrey Chaucer*, 2d ed. (Boston:
Houghton Mifflin, 1957), p. 267.

4

The Question of Unity

The *Parlement of Foules*

This chapter looks directly at a question that no critical study can ignore and that we have in fact alluded to repeatedly in the preceding chapters. The *Parlement of Foules* is an especially suitable text for studying the idea of unity, since so much of the critical commentary is devoted to "discovering" the poem's unity. The effort has been sufficiently concerted to justify the inference that such unity is not only problematical but perhaps even imaginary. J. A. W. Bennett's impatient utterance— "If we assume that it has no organic unity . . . then we had better close our Chaucer and open our *Reader's Digest*"[1]—represents the critical view that has dominated modern commentary until recently, when some dissenting voices have been raised. More than the *Book of the Duchess* and the *House of Fame*, the *Parlement* has attracted defenders of its unity, though as we have seen, those works too have had their share of unifiers. Perhaps because the *Parlement* is somewhat more densely textured than the earlier poems, it has exerted a special appeal to critics who share the Coleridgian and New Critical predilection for paradoxically unified oppositions and subtly connected images. The burden of the present chapter will be to demonstrate that such a model is alien to the actual properties of the *Parlement* and that the poem can live and thrive on its own terms.

The quest for unity often takes the form of interpretation, in the sense that Tzvetan Todorov distinguishes from poetics

---

1. J. A. W. Bennett, *The Parlement of Foules: An Interpretation* (Oxford: Clarendon Press, 1957), pp. 15–16.

or analysis, as we have noted. As an ideal condition unity has always been associated in the Western mind with perfection, and the boundary between the perfect ideal and imperfect but aspiring actualities is thin and porous and often subject to wishful interpretation. In literary studies the power of the idea can sweep obstructions aside and create unified edifices of interpretive thought that may bear only slight relation to textual actualities. Gérard Genette defines the critical issue unequivocally: "It would be unfortunate, it seems to me, to seek 'unity' at any price, and in that way to *force* the work's coherence—which is, of course, one of criticism's strongest temptations, one of its most ordinary (not to say most common) ones, and also one most easy to satisfy, since all it requires is a little interpretative rhetoric."[2] Too often the quest for unity leads either up the high metaphorical road to a unity in the critic's mind (or in God's) or down the low profound road to a unity in the collective unconscious. Either way the tendency is toward a nonliterary reductionism that devalues the artistic text. By resolving discords into harmony, the critic is able to demonstrate—at least to his own satisfaction—that a highly valued, though apparently erratic or inconsistent, text is indeed unified. The tendency of unitary interpretation is to deny diversity, to interpret it out, so to speak, in order to certify the value of an admired text. It is not unusual for the eager critic to assert that his text is, say, an expression of the Christian doctrine of charity, or a rendering of the Oedipal relationship, or a chronicle of modern suburbia, or an analogue of the romantic quest that in turn is a version of the myth of eternal renewal. By such means the value of a text is derived from extratextual prototypes that are presumed to be more exalted or more profound than the text itself. By referring his text to a supratextual ideal, the interpretive critic preempts the need for textual analysis. Such a procedure places a high premium on ideological, paraphrasable meaning, but in so doing it pays the price Genette refers to. It scants the tex-

2. Gérard Genette, *Narrative Discourse: An Essay in Method,* trans. Jane E. Lewin (Ithaca, N.Y.: Cornell Univ. Press, 1980), p. 266.

tual actualities, "imperfections" and all, that differentiate literary art from other forms of communication. Insofar as interpretation seeks to measure a work's value by demonstrating its adherence to a higher or lower unitary model, it proceeds to create its own world of discourse. In that endeavor interpretation is likely to prove dispensable. Either it will itself become poetry, or it must finally acknowledge the ineffability of the primary text.

The alternative I wish to pursue with respect to the *Parlement of Foules* entails suspension of the twofold presupposition that unity is a condition necessary to literary value and that it is derivable, by way of thematic interpretation, from extraliterary concepts. If we suspend the unitary presupposition, a fresh analysis of the text may admit the possibility of discovering within the poet's system of language a principle of order other than what we designate—often loosely and arbitrarily—by the eulogistic term *unity*. The object of analysis so conducted is to discover principles both intrinsic to literary art and primarily aesthetic, in contrast to principles derived extrinsically by way of referential interpretation.

The *Parlement of Foules* shares with the other dream visions, the *Troilus*, and the tales of Canterbury, both individually and in the aggregate, a quality of internal variousness that has proven especially challenging to criticism; the profusion of unity studies indicates the *Parlement*'s resistance to unitary interpretation. Crowded as it is with contrasts and irregularities on every level and in every aspect—mixed styles, varied and incongruous subjects, contradictory authorial attitudes—this poem defies seekers after its unifying principle. Dorothy Bethurum formulated the overwhelming question when she asked, "Where is the unity in a poem which begins with a résumé of Cicero's *Somnium Scipionis* . . . and proceeds to a love-*debat*?"[3] The search has been conducted largely along thematic lines, and many of the searchers have themselves been uneasy with their findings. Bertrand Bronson finds that

---

3. Dorothy Bethurum, "The Center of the *Parlement of Foules*," in *Essays in Honor of Walter Clyde Curry*, Vanderbilt Studies in the Humanities, vol. 2 (Nashville, Tenn.: Vanderbilt Univ. Press, 1955), p. 48.

the poem's belittling of things temporal in contrast with things eternal provides "moral depth and responsibility, a sound and coherent structure."[4] Yet Bronson recognizes, almost in the same breath, the inadequacy of his formulation, for moral depth and coherence are denied by the poem's "unabashed lightness of heart." In the end he declares the work "too nimble for criticism." In other words, its unity eludes us, as Bethurum also attests when she admits she cannot answer her question. Yet she makes the effort. Like Bronson, she adopts a thematic interpretation. Arguing that the work is a "love poem" about "fertility and generation," she maintains therefore that "the Garden of Love is central to the poem and gives design to all the rest" (pp. 39–40). In view of the obvious claims of other parts of the poem,[5] Bethurum's claim for the garden is plainly tendentious, uttered more in hope, one feels, than in conviction. Donald Baker agrees with Bethurum that the garden is the heart of the poem, but he feels none the wiser for that: "I shall begin by confessing that I am not at all sure what the *Parliament* is about."[6] Following this disclaimer, Baker's effort to discern a unifying principle is predictably weak. Summing up his account of the poem's diversities, he asserts that "the poem's parts blend . . . in an affirmation of human worth" (p. 366).

While the *Parlement*'s diversities have thwarted thematic unifiers, they have proven equally intractable in several structurally oriented studies. Wolfgang Clemen notes with considerable precision important aspects of the poem's variousness: "Instead of uniformity, his [Chaucer's] diction and presentation display a varied, richly contrasting gradation."[7] But Clemen nevertheless feels the need to unify, to discover some-

---

4. Bertrand H. Bronson, *In Search of Chaucer* (Toronto: Univ. of Toronto Press, 1960), p. 46.

5. Wolfgang Clemen, for example, regards the garden not as the poem's center but as a "prelude" to the parliament (*Chaucer's Early Poetry*, trans. C. A. M. Sym [London: Methuen, 1963], p. 143).

6. Donald C. Baker, "The Parliament of Fowls," in *Companion to Chaucer Studies*, ed. Beryl Rowland, rev. ed. (New York: Oxford Univ. Press, 1979), p. 435.

7. Clemen, *Chaucer's Early Poetry*, p. 169.

thing more satisfying behind the text's rough surface. His effort on this score verges on the mystical: "Behind this surface-relationship, more essential links are forged, most of which Chaucer allows us only to guess at" (p. 128). Brewer reaches a similarly vague conclusion, seeing the poem finally as "a complex whole of related thoughts, feelings, and experiences . . . where there is a place for many things."[8]

Another school of unifying thought would in effect bypass the question by referring it to the nature of dreams. In a book aptly entitled *The Realism of Dream Visions*, Constance Hieatt seeks the unity of the poem in the unity of its presumed referent: "A good part of this unity can be attributed to the fact that the poem is a dream, and follows, like Chaucer's other dream visions, a specific dream logic."[9] The problem here is the easy assertion that "the poem is a dream." A moment's reflection tells us that dreams—even Freud's own, I have no doubt—do not display the finely tuned rhetoric and sustained verbal articulation that we encounter in a Chaucerian dream vision. The poem is not a dream but an artful verbal composition that effects the *illusion* of a dream as a formal framing device. The illusion is not developed realistically; the poem's referential object, in other words, cannot be reduced to a dream. The poem refers to many things, among them old books, new poems, love and the language of lovers, and the labor itself of writing. The unity of "dream logic"—even supposing there is such a thing—can tell us very little about Chaucer's poem.

A pattern is evident in these approaches to the problem of unity: the poem's contrasts, incongruities, even contradictions are clearly evident to the discerning eye, but unity remains beyond reach. It is regularly asserted to exist but nowhere demonstrated persuasively and with confidence. In relation to this palpably various—and typically Chaucerian—

---

8. Derek S. Brewer, ed., *The Parlement of Foulys* (London: Nelson, 1960), p. 25.

9. Constance Hieatt, *The Realism of Dream Visions* (The Hague: Mouton, 1967), p. 78.

poem the term *unity* cannot claim precision of meaning. It seems simply to imply a quality that is assumed both to be artistically necessary and to determine the order of an admired poem. Lacking a persuasive "unification" of such a poem, we need not conclude that it is inferior or disorderly. Indeed, the attention it continues to command attests to its value. But neither should we assume that we shall eventually discover its unity if we only try hard enough. The problem, I think, is a faulty conception of what we are seeking. In other words, we are faced not with a bad poem or with faulty critical observation but with a failure of theory. We have not developed a model, an idea of poetic form, to which we can satisfactorily refer this poem. I think the formulation of such a model depends on our willingness to entertain some hitherto unpopular possibilities:

1. that the poem's loose, irregular surface might not be as deceptive as we have thought, that it might mean what it says, however inconsistent and multivocal;
2. that the poem might not in fact possess the unity we have been seeking;
3. that the poem may be aesthetically none the worse and perhaps even somewhat the better for that.

The essential first step toward such a reassessment was taken by Arthur Moore in an important article that deserves the attention of all medievalists who profess to criticism of literary texts.[10] After reviewing the necessary and sufficient conditions for any theory of unity, Moore demonstrates the practical consequences of inadequate theory in the criticism of *Beowulf*, *Piers Plowman*, and the *Morte Darthur*, with a penetrating glance at the *Parlement* and the *Canterbury Tales* as well. His analysis of the "unchecked flow of unity studies" leads to the conclusion that "the use of the term *unity* is essentially valuational rather than descriptive . . . a means of enhancing

---

10. Arthur K. Moore, "Medieval English Literature and the Question of Unity," *Modern Philology* 65 (1968): 285–300.

the value of numerous medieval poems and prose works well beyond previous estimations" (p. 300). Moore's article reminds us that a priori models must accord with inferences legitimately derived from the evidence of the text and that if they do not, then other models must be discovered or at least acknowledged to exist. To discover models suitable to the facts of medieval narrative is a difficult matter, as *Parlement* criticism illustrates. But once the theoretical ground is cleared, the construction of a coherent and useful model becomes easier.

Some relevant and helpful advances in this direction have been made by students of Old French metrical romances and prose cycles. William Ryding devotes a chapter of his book on structure in medieval narrative to "the question of unity."[11] Acknowledging a certain validity in the concepts of unity defined by theme (for example, quest, love, moral struggle) or by the pervasive presence of a hero (Renart, Lancelot), Ryding nevertheless reaches conclusions consonant with Moore's dissatisfaction with the "vague focus" such definitions provide. Such theories are too thin to cover the textual realities that emerge when a narrative is examined in sharper focus. Ryding observes that "we seldom stop to consider whether there might not be some advantage in relinquishing the idea of unity altogether and admitting at least hypothetically the validity of artistic duality, trinity, or some other form of multiplicity" (p. 115). Despite our reluctance to abandon the unitary model, there is ample evidence, not only in medieval literary works themselves but in the writings of medieval theorists, as Ryding points out, to suggest that medieval writers were persuaded that "the secret of elegance lay not in the unification of the matter but rather in the multiplication of its elements" (pp. 115–16).

Similar observations have been made by Eugène Vinaver: "'Organic unity,' in the sense in which we commonly use the term, turns out to be a metaphor whose validity is strictly lim-

---

11. William W. Ryding, *Structure in Medieval Narrative* (The Hague: Mouton, 1971).

ited in time, and it is our failure to grasp this simple fact that has caused us to overlook the very things that give life and meaning to medieval literary art." [12] These very things are multiplicity, repetition, and above all acentricity, resulting in "cohesion without unity." Vinaver is thinking primarily of French prose romances and aesthetic analogues in Romanesque ornamentation, but his observations are also useful for the student of Chaucerian narrative.

Another source of broader theoretical perspective has been the work of certain art historians. In a general way Heinrich Wölfflin established the basis for alternatives when he differentiated between "multiple unity" and "unified unity," the one associated with the "linear" style, the other with the "painterly." A characteristic passage from Wölfflin will suggest how much his insights have influenced the principal theoretical distinctions I have been drawing in this book. He is distinguishing between two modes of portraiture:

> In Holbein the forms stand side by side as independent and relatively coordinated values, while in Frans Hals or Velasquez certain groups of forms take the lead, the whole is subordinated to a definite motive of movement or expression, and in this combination the details can no longer assert an existence of their own. . . . The [painterly] effect is not based on the juxtaposition of separate forms, but rather on the whole as a whole, subjected to a leading motive and the uniform accentuation of the members as isolated parts [is] surrendered. . . . For the beauty of the classic [linear] style, the uniformly clear visibility of all the parts is the *sine qua non*. [13]

The concept of "multiple unity" that Wölfflin finds exemplified in Holbein offers a significant alternative to the Velasquez-like "unified unity" that critics have been seeking in the *Parlement*. Most of my ensuing discussion of the *Parlement* will be concerned with expounding the "linear" clarity of its juxtaposed

---

12. Eugène Vinaver, *The Rise of Romance* (Oxford: Clarendon Press, 1971), p. 77.
13. Heinrich Wölfflin, *Principles of Art History*, trans. M. D. Hottinger, 7th ed. (Germany, 1915; New York: Dover, n.d.), pp. 167, 169. See also pp. 18–20, 155–63.

rhetorical forms and the correlation between the observable features of the text and the idea of "multiple unity."

In his celebrated tour de force *Gothic Architecture and Scholasticism* Erwin Panofsky shows how the theoretical distinctions Wölfflin propounds can illuminate verbal arts.[14] By viewing the scholastic *summa* as a structure of verbal materials, shaped and disposed in analogy with the shaping and disposition of materials in a Gothic cathedral, Panofsky provides a critical vocabulary that can be applied to other verbal structures as well, such as narrative poems. Panofsky clarifies the concept of quantitative textuality by comparing the structural principles observed in common by verbal forms and architectural forms.[15] Awareness of the palpability of verbal forms brings us back to rhetoric and a concept the Middle Ages understood very well, as we have seen in Boccaccio and medieval rhetoricians and in the conventional metaphor of the text as an adorned garment. With the help of modern theoretical studies we are extending our vision beyond the Jamesian and neo-Coleridgian model of the transparent text and extratextual, ideal unity and rediscovering the rhetorical model of mixed forms in an aggregative whole.

Chaucerians too have begun to question the presupposition behind unity hunting and to explore new alternatives. Derek Brewer, for example, has proposed that "in the light of modern

14. Erwin Panofsky, *Gothic Architecture and Scholasticism* (1951; reprint, New York: Meridian Books, 1957).

15. Panofsky defines these common principles as (1) totality, (2) arrangement according to a system of homologous parts and parts of parts, and (3) distinctness of articulation, all serving, according to the principle of *manifestatio*, or "clarification for clarification's sake," to elucidate the processes of both verbal and architectural construction (pp. 31–35). In an earlier study of the *Parlement*, extensively revised here, I borrowed Panofsky's method and applied the principle of *manifestatio* to the poem ("The Question of Unity and the *Parlement of Foules*," *English Studies in Canada* 3 [1977]: 373–85). For a detailed development of the analogy between Gothic architecture and *Troilus* and the *Canterbury Tales* see my *Chaucer and the Shape of Creation* (Cambridge: Harvard Univ. Press, 1967), pp. 44–110. See also Derek S. Brewer, "Gothic Chaucer," in *Geoffrey Chaucer*, ed. Derek S. Brewer (London: Bell, 1974), pp. 1–32. For a strong argument in favor of replacing "Gothic" with "Menippean" in this literary usage see F. Anne Payne, *Chaucer and Menippean Satire* (Madison: Univ. of Wisconsin Press, 1981), p. 266.

experience and a contemplation of fourteenth-century culture, we . . . abandon the attempt to discover a relatively
simply unified, non-Gothic, dominant pattern in the literary
culture represented by Chaucer's works and their social circumstances."[16] Similarly, Stewart Justman has argued that
Chaucer's many appeals to traditional authorities are often
contradictory: "Not only do the authorities fail to unify the
world of Chaucer's creation, they emphasize its disunity."[17]
John McCall has addressed the question of the *Parlement*'s
unity, pointedly suggesting that "we may have been looking
and listening for the wrong things."[18] His article establishes a
rationale for accepting the poem's clashes and dissonances, its
"jarring rhetorical patterns," as the "earthly music" they are,
harmonized ultimately, McCall maintains, under the aspect
of divine order. H. Marshall Leicester questions the utility
and also the validity of McCall's summoning heavenly harmony and the familiar *discordia concors* idea to explain the
poem, though he too acknowledges the poem's dissonances.[19]
Leicester argues that the great cosmic synthesis expounded
by Alanus and many another "auctoritee" and paraphrased
by Chaucer in the early stanzas of the *Parlement* was already
breaking down in the fourteenth century. He sees the *Parlement* as a record of Chaucer's personal, subjective responses
to the "multiplicity, richness and variety of the authoritative
traditions, conventions, literary models, lore, etc." (p. 18)
that he knew in his culture. In the course of his discussion
Leicester raises some of the important theoretical questions
about Chaucer's poetics that bear on our subject. Leicester
stresses, for example, the poem's reflexive reminders of its
make-believe, craftsmanly quality and its "recreative verbal

16. "Gothic Chaucer," in Brewer, *Geoffrey Chaucer*, p. 12.

17. Stewart Justman, "Medieval Monism and the Abuse of Authority in
Chaucer," *Chaucer Review* 11 (1976): 96. See also his citation (p. 111) of Delany
and Brewer on Chaucer's "multivalent tradition" and the need for "pluralistic" modes of interpretation.

18. John P. McCall, "The Harmony of Chaucer's *Parliament*," *Chaucer Review* 5 (1970): 22–31.

19. H. Marshall Leicester, Jr., "The Harmony of Chaucer's *Parlement*: A
Dissonant Voice," *Chaucer Review* 9 (1974): 15–34.

play of imitation *qua* imitation, with minimal concern for the expressive value, objective content, or wider relevance of the poem to the forms imitated" (p. 21). Leicester comes to no unitary conclusion but rather draws a sensitive picture of a richly complex poem not firmly convinced of its own values and equally unsure about the conventional authority it calls on to harmonize the discords of earthly experience.

In an equally provocative departure from the presuppositions of the unity studies, David Aers expresses admiration for much of Leicester's essay but questions the basis for some of his socio-cultural claims.[20] Aers makes his own case for the "total disappearance of traditionally 'authoritative' instructors in Chaucer's works" (p. 9). He argues that the *Parlement* juxtaposes pagan (Neoplatonic) authority against Christian "in a process which is thoroughly subversive of *all* forms of dogmatic thought." In the *Parlement* Chaucer evolves "a literary form which resists confident metaphysical assertions about 'The wey to come into that hevene blisse' (72), presenting us with a dynamic world of conflicting interests and multiple viewpoints where no one can even claim access to an absolute and impersonal viewpoint, from which to issue timelessly valid 'authoritative' statements" (p. 8).

In effect Aers and Leicester provide a persuasive epistemological rationale for the "disunity" of the *Parlement*. In so doing they establish a more sophisticated critical groundwork than the unity studies assume, one that is also truer to the observable features of the poem. No longer predirected by unitary assumptions, analysis can proceed from a study of the poem's manifest features to derive the system of order—the poetics—that governs its form. In its particular way, as we shall see, the *Parlement* expresses the fundamental ambivalence that energizes the *Book of the Duchess* and the *House of Fame*, the ambivalence of fixed and authoritative verbal forms whose ontological validity is questionable.

The *Parlement* is not a tightly reasoned or finely balanced

20. David Aers, "The *Parliament of Fowls*: Authority, the Knower, and the Known," *Chaucer Review* 16 (1981): 1–17.

work. Its texture, like that of much medieval poetry, is loose rather than dense; it is diffuse, not concentrated; and it is explicit rather than subtly allusive. In other words, it is not a metaphysical lyric or a "well-made novel" and cannot be expected to respond to critical criteria appropriate to such forms. The *Parlement* divides into sections, or rhetorical blocks, almost as diversified in content, style, and perspective as the sections of the *House of Fame*. Robert Frank has drawn convenient broad distinctions between moralistic prelude, conventional love garden, and realistic debate,[21] but it should not be presumed that these are self-consistent parts. In the craftsmanly, self-conscious mode of the poem, consistency of texture frequently and often unexpectedly gives way to digressive and prolix displays of erudition, such as the prominent inventories of birds, trees, and legendary lovers. Similarly, the poem's stylistic diversity is often more a demonstration of dazzling virtuosity for its own sake than an organic complement of significant inner meaning. Although analytical partitioning helps us to see that the text consists of many things, we should also recognize the importance of the structural principle of coordination. The parts and parts of parts are not subordinate to a larger "idea" but rather enjoy individual completeness and equal worth within the frame of the poem. This is the principle that Wölfflin discerns in the "linear" style of portraiture and that Bethurum and others fail to recognize in their search for the "center" of the poem. As we shall see, the poem has no center.

From the outset the poem's movement is dilatory, spasmodic, marked by abrupt and surprising shifts of subject, style, and authorial attitude. The opening lines strike a tone of solemnity and high moral purpose on the theme of *ars longa, vita brevis*:

> The lyf so short, the craft so long to lerne,
> Th'assay so hard, so sharp the conquerynge,
> The dredful joye, alwey that slit so yerne:
>
> (1–3)

21. Robert W. Frank, Jr., "Structure and Meaning in the *Parlement of Foules*," *PMLA* 71 (1956): 530–39.

But from this philosophical height Chaucer quickly drops to the bathos. Defying the connotative weight of these opening lines, the speaker states flatly in the next line that he is talking about Love—the cruel and capricious god, that is, whose wonderful workings so dazzle him that he scarcely knows whether he floats or sinks. Thus in a single seven-line stanza Chaucer swings from high seriousness to comic self-parody and in so doing signals the wide cognitive and stylistic range of the poem as well as its unpredictable mode of development.

In the second stanza, rather than attempt to salvage something of the moral and philosophical connotations of Love, the narrator clings to the courtly idiom and converts it to bathos with a comic display of his own unlikeliness as a lover and his credulous subservience to that imperious lord:

> For al be that I knowe nat Love in dede,
> Ne wot how that he quiteth folk here hyre,
> Yit happeth me ful ofte in bokes reede
> Of his myrakles and his crewel yre.
> There rede I wel he wol be lord and syre;
> I dar nat seyn, his strokes been so sore,
> But "God save swich a lord!"—I can na moore.
>
> (8–14)

Following this parodic introduction of courtly postures, the poem once more abruptly changes direction. Executing a quick pivot on the word "bokes" (having said he knows about Love only from what he has read in books), the speaker proceeds to describe his reading habits. And then he asks, rhetorically, "But wherfore that I speke al this?" (l. 17). Wherefore, indeed, we might echo, for he goes on to paraphrase, without explanation, not a book of Cupid's deeds, or even a book of lovers (of which Chaucer knew many, including his Ovid and the *Romance of the Rose*), but a work of high moral and cosmic speculation, the *Somnium Scipionis*. The next sixty lines of the poem are essentially a paraphrase of this work, treated seriously and with respect for its moral content. This part of the poem is virtually an autonomous narrative, a detailed account of Africanus's journey through the heavenly spheres to "that blysful place" to which will proceed all those who while on earth pursue the common weal. Its characters are historical personages; its setting is the Platonic cosmos; and its concern is moral philosophy. Although this part of the poem is perfectly coherent in itself, its relevance to what precedes and follows it is by no means self-evident. The only apparent link between the god of Love and Scipio Africanus is that the narrator's knowledge of both came from books. The connection is not logically compelling, and we would do well to acknowledge this rather than argue for a more organic fusion. Further, we should recognize the possibility that this looser connectivity might be the norm of Chaucer's compositional procedure, an idea supported by our study of the *House of Fame* and the *Book of the Duchess.*

This sequence of passages—the sententious opening lines, the comic mock-adulation of Cupid, the long, serious paraphrase of Cicero—establishes the mixed mode of the poem. Some readers will regard the allusion to the god of Love, and the accompanying tone of mock adulation, as a momentary digression, a bit of comic relief sandwiched between the sententious opening and the sympathetic rendering of Cicero. Others, more bent on discovering comic unity in the poem, will regard this comic moment as a foretaste of raucous moments to come. To build an interpretive case for the unifying idea of the poem—whether sententious or comic, moral or skeptical—requires a satisfactory definiton of the base from which divergence can be measured. And that, of course, is precisely the problem.

It is difficult to determine which strain is primary—solemn sententiousness or comic skepticism. And Chaucer seems to delight in thwarting the desire to reconcile or "unify." Robert Frank has defined the pattern of the poem's movement as "failure of expectation,"[22] a justifiable assessment that recognizes Chaucer's elusiveness, his resistance to committing his art to a single purpose or theme or verbal style. The sequence we are considering thus suggests another working hypothesis for our appraisal of the *Parlement* as a whole, namely that the poem is acentric, that its "unity" is not single but multiple,

22. Frank, "Structure and Meaning," p. 537.

and that any a priori notion of a "unifying principle" is likely
to ignore or subordinate parts that are diverse, recalcitrant, or
mutually contradictory but that nevertheless assert valid and
lively claims to our attention. We see, then, that the first ninety
lines, about one-eighth of the poem, do not refer to a parliament or to birds—the ostensible "central" subject of the
poem—or even to a garden but rather present a mixed gathering of subjects and styles.

In a transitional passage following his summary of the
Somnium Scipionis the narrator explains how he took to his
bed when daylight failed. A major division of the poem is
clearly articulated at line 95 as the narrator, having finally
fallen asleep, begins the account of his wonderful dream with
the sudden appearance of Africanus, who guides him to the
garden of love. This account in turn divides into two principal
sections, the description of the garden, which extends for
some two hundred lines, and the parliament of birds in the
final four hundred lines of the poem.

We need not dwell on the description of the garden except
to note that it is a richly detailed example of rhetorical elucidation. The love personifications—Plesaunce, Curteysie,
and so forth—exemplify the impulse to elucidate as they display the elements of aristocratic love in vivid and explicit form.
The sharply wrought figures of the gods and goddesses serve
a similar purpose, and Chaucer further extends the proce-
dures of clarification and display with an assortment of the
traditional images of the love garden—flowers, meadows,
sweetly singing birds, "bestes smale of gentil kynde," "smale
fishes lite," and so forth. All of these materials, combined
with similarly pictorialized materials on the walls of Venus's
temple, impart to the garden section qualities that are primarily visual and spectacular. Animate as well as inanimate
figures are individually depicted, arrested in characteristic attitudes and framed in a nonrealistic configuration. The quality
of formal display is underscored by the absence of significant
interplay among the figures in the garden: all face outward, so
to speak, toward the viewer. In the sharp articulation of its
component elements as well as in its impulse toward inclu-

siveness and totality of enumeration, the garden scene exemplifies features of Gothic style that Panofsky has identified
in the structure of cathedral and *summa*, as I have already
noted.[23]

Although Chaucer draws some lines of continuity, the relation between the garden section and the parliament section
that follows it (beginning in l. 295) is in many respects one of
discontinuity. The sections are individuated and contiguous;
they are not successive stages in an evolving development.
For example, nothing in the frieze-like garden section pre-
pares us for the noise and the broiling "humanity" of the parliament. These talking birds are a different order of being entirely from the stylized avian figures of the garden section.
We have noted from the very beginning how abruptly and unexpectedly the poem moves—from the cosmic to the human,
the general to the personal, the solemn to the comic, with
styles and attitudes appropriately diverse. In the present instance the garden section and the parliament section bear a
loose thematic relation—they are versions of secular love or,
more properly speaking, love language—but in the sharper
focus of aesthetic and structural analysis the relation is primarily one of simple contiguity as each section proceeds to its
independent presentation, not without some overlap and
contradiction. Although my aim in this analysis is not to trace
literary "influences," it is plain that a major progenitor of the
garden section is Guillaume's part of the *Roman de la rose*.

Though it too is a vehicle for literary elucidation and display, the parliament section differs from the garden section as
profoundly as Jean de Meun does from Guillaume, and the
relationship between sections is similarly loose and juxtaposi-
tional rather than integral and logical, the main connecting
device being the minimal presence of the narrator in both sections. The parliament section is dramatic in contrast to the descriptive character of the garden, and this is part of the discontinuous relation I have been describing. But in a larger
sense the "drama" of the parliament serves the same exposi-

23. See note 15 above.

tory purpose as the spectacle of the garden. It too pursues the aim of rhetorical display, which it fulfills by marshaling the languages of love, courtly, common, and mixed, and casting them in a dialogue of comically discordant voices.

It is fitting that Nature should arrange the jostling birds in a hierarchical scale, thus providing a framework for distinct articulation of elements and inclusive enumeration. As in much medieval schematizing, the idea of *schema* is more important than empirical verification of the *differentiae,* and in this instance Chaucer uses the schematic framework to support an encyclopedic enumeration of the known birds of the world, not very carefully differentiated according to hierarchical ranks in every case but satisfyingly complete. "What shulde I seyne?" asks the awestruck narrator in the midst of his enumerative efforts,

> Of foules every kynde
> That in this world han fetheres and stature
> Men myghten in that place assembled fynde
> Byfore the noble goddesse of Nature.
>
> (365–68)

The hierarchical ordering of the birds is another manifestation of the controlling procedural principles of fine articulation and fullness of enumeration: whether in their avian terms—birds of prey, worm eaters, waterfowl, seed eaters—or in their implied correlative strata of social estates, the scope is comprehensive and the exemplary figures are clearly individuated. The three noble suitors for the hand (claw) of the gentle formel are endowed with suitable aristocratic bearing and courtly speech.

An important structural ambiguity arises in the relation between the three royal suitors and the narrative context in which the debate is set. These courtiers display *in extenso* the love language of the chivalric ethos. They thus constitute a repetition in different form of the values represented by pictorial means in the garden section. While this varied repetition is consistent with an aesthetic that emphasizes fullness of elucidation, it also produces some striking discontinuities. First, the fictive characterization of these courting birds bears no relation to the stylized birds that fill the trees in the garden section, "with voys of aungel in here armonye." Second, the courtly ethos that is absolute in the garden scene is relative, to say the least, in the parliament. Although designated the highest in degree (l. 394), the courtly viewpoint is exposed to refutation, if not ridicule, in the parliament section. The comic skepticism contrasts utterly with the veneration of the same values in the preceding section.

The noisy debate among the lower birds is thoroughly engaging for its "human" touches, not the least of which is the inability of these impatient debaters to sustain the logical course of an argument. But we should note that the digressiveness and the logical inconsistencies are aesthetically consistent with the poem's aggregative compositional structure. Earlier the poem had pictorialized the silent abstractions of Plesaunce, Curteysie, Delyt, and the rest ad libitum; here the impulse to analyze and display is developed in a different way. Here the figures are not arrested in frozen, silent gestures but rather are given both movement and voice. Moreover, they engage with one another, unlike the figures in the garden section. This artistic illusion is so entirely different that it raises once again the question of narrative unity. Can a poem possess unity when its parts follow structural principles that differ fundamentally from one another?

The structural differences between the garden and the parliament sections are defined in part by the role of the narrator. In the garden section the narrator is relatively prominent. His directly reported observations, accentuated by the repeated use of "I," serve as a frame to capture and enclose the scene. In the parliament section, however, he is inconspicuous; he is absorbed, so to speak, into the scene itself from the moment he finds a place to stand among the crowd of those present. As a result, in the absence of a narrating "I" for almost two hundred lines (ll. 493–679), the illusion is one of openness, unframed and unmediated. This is the kind of narrative situation we find in the most intensely emotional sections of *Troilus and Criseyde,* where the lover's anxiety and suffering are not mediated by a narrator who is conspicuous elsewhere in the poem.[24] In the present instance the emotional tone bespeaks no anxiety or personal suffering, but the controlling viewpoint of the narrative, which determines the nature of the illusion and the nature of the viewer's (or reader's) relationship to the illusion, differs distinctly from that elsewhere in the poem.

On such dramatic interplay of individualized voices rests much of Chaucer's popular reputation as an earthy and realistic poet. We should recognize, however, both in the *Parlement* and in the *Canterbury Tales*, where Chaucer explores this mode more fully, that the "realistic" illusion is momentary and partial. It is one of many literary resources or options available to a poet working within a rhetorical poetics. When the artistic aim is not to blend fiction with life but rather to celebrate the medium and display its literary possibilities, the range of expressiveness broadens. Paradoxically, this extended range of expressiveness depends on a strictly delimited sense of artistic illusion. That is, the poet understands himself to be essentially a craftsman and only partially a magician, as the ending of the *Parlement* reminds us.

Before considering the ending we should make one or two further observations about the parliament section. The failure of the debate itself to reach a resolution of the arguments so extensively, if sometimes deviously, developed is one more instance of the poem's indifference to imperatives of unitary resolution. But while the formel makes no choice at all, the other birds are quickly mated. The perfunctory quality of this resolution, as well as its irrelevance to the debate that occupies so much of the parliament section, makes clear that in the structural mode of this poem it is less important to resolve conflicting forces than to accommodate their full display within the poem's elastic frame. The attempt to resolve the ethical differences between courtly and "natural" values into a triumph of *Natura*, as represented by the mass matings and the joyous roundel—that is, the attempt to render unitary what Chaucer

---

24. For a discussion of this effect in *Troilus* see my *Chaucer and the Shape of Creation*, pp. 92–94.

presents as multiple—is unjustifiably arbitrary and subjective. Aers enforces this point when he argues that "only a reading, determined to dissolve the particulars of Chaucer's art and contexts, would attempt to take this ending as an authoritative image of metaphysical and cosmic harmony coherently ordering apparent conflict into a unified totality."[25] I think Aers overstates the point, however, when he goes on to assert that "Chaucer's mode is utterly subversive of all attempts to substitute impersonal knowledge and an absolute viewpoint for the complex processes involving incarnate and historically specific 'knowers'" (p. 14). The fervor of this assertion is misleading, for it imparts to the poem an ideological purposefulness that dispassionate analysis fails to confirm. Being before all else a poet, Chaucer deserves a primary assessment that does full justice to his poetic sensibility, to the choices he makes in selecting and composing the materials of his art. From this point of view the *Parlement*'s epistemological ambivalence is an attribute of a poetics that offers a multiplicity of "authoritative" models and generic and stylistic choices. Chaucer is better understood, I think, as a pluralistic poet than as a "subversive" philosopher.

Following the dispersal of the parliament, the poem ends not with an outcome but with a conclusion. The distinction is important because it marks the difference between a work that follows the imperatives of logical, sequential development and one like the *Parlement* that follows a disjunct, presentational model. The ending of the *Parlement*, as Leicester and Aers both point out, reminds us self-reflexively of the poem's crafted status. The narrator's framing voice reasserts itself, humorously puncturing the dream illusion with an "explanation" of the roundel:

> The note, I trowe, imaked was in Fraunce,
> The wordes were swiche as ye may heer fynde,
> The nexte vers, as I now have in mynde.
>
> (677–79)

---

25. Aers, "The *Parliament*," p. 14.

This imaginary garden, we are told, is peopled by real birds who sing in English a song composed in France. Such sophisticated playfulness—collapsing levels of illusion and homogenizing absolutely differentiated states of being—depends on a high degree of literary consciousness and an appreciation of the artistry and play of literary illusion.

The ending of the *Parlement* is as gratuitous and externalized as the ending of the parliamentary debate. Neither is the result of interior forces moving compellingly to a logical outcome. The awakening of the narrator and his reassertion of himself as a writer and reader is an externally imposed return to the beginning. As such it suitably frames the narrative without betraying any necessary internal relations with it. Within that frame the *Parlement* presents an array of poetic entities largely independent of one another in subject matter, style, characters, even fictional mode: from the opening stanzas in which Chaucer swings ambivalently between sententious philosophizing and comic self-deflation; to the paraphrase of the *Somnium Scipionis* and its philosophical and moral vision of the cosmos; to the lavish presentation of the earthly garden of love, where the style and imagery are courtly and the characters are silent personifications; and finally to the avian parliament, where the materials are common as well as aristocratic and the characters are loquacious birds. Crowding all of these diverse elements and more within its brief compass, the *Parlement* subordinates narrative continuity to a mode of presentation that is expository and spatial rather than developmental and temporal. Since the parts of the poem are so diverse, and since each part is developed in its own terms and without primacy over the others, the *Parlement* is in fact a poem without a center and without a denouement. In other words, it does not satisfy the requirements of aesthetic unity as that idea is conventionally understood. It does, however, have a circumference, affirmed by self-reflexive allusions (most prominent at beginning and end) to its status as a literary whole composed as conscious make-believe and encompassing a variety of literary and cultural traditions. While many commentators have regarded love as the source of unity in the poem, such a source exists largely outside the work, and the search for it leaves the poem itself in vague focus.

In the sharp focus in which we have attempted to examine it, the *Parlement* reveals itself to be a mixture of remarkably various parts. Such a structure is not accurately defined by reference to an "organic" model, for it lacks the single unifying impulse, the continuous development, and above all the economy of means that would ensure tightness of structure and the relevance of all parts. It exhibits instead the formal attributes of discontinuity and acentricity, and it tends not to economy and relevance but to variegated, encyclopedic display. We find it difficult to comprehend a poem whose parts are so sharply articulated, so various, and so loosely integrated. But rather than try to reconcile disparities and file down sharp edges to squeeze the poem into a particular form of unity, we are better advised to recognize the limits of organicism and the possibilities of a different aesthetic, one that values conscious artifice and embraces a multiplicity of rhetorical styles and epistemological viewpoints. The rediscovery and re-articulation of such a poetics by postmodernist writers and critics lends support, as we have seen, to the efforts of Chaucerians to understand and justify the poet's achievement according to criteria that are both valid and appropriate. In reflecting such criteria the *Parlement* is more typical than unique among Chaucer's works. Its "multiple unity" recalls the structure of the dream visions that preceded its composition and anticipates a fundamental ordering principle of the *Legend of Good Women* and the *Canterbury Tales*.

5

The Limits of Self-Parody

The Prologue to the *Legend of Good Women*

Compared with the other dream visions and the vigorous interpretive controversies they have generated, the Prologue to the *Legend of Good Women* has attracted a modest amount of critical attention.[1] The absent testimony lends support to the somewhat negative argument I want to advance, namely that the Prologue did not fully engage Chaucer's artistic interest. The result is a poem difficult to come to terms with. It displays the characteristic Chaucerian features of a rhetorically conceived, self-reflexive, generically and stylistically mixed poem, yet all these features are uncharacteristically muted, and the whole enterprise exhibits an unusual restraint. The poem is less multivalent (and therefore less "controversial") than the others we have considered, but despite its comparatively narrow range it does not submit easily to unitary interpretation.

As a dream vision the Prologue differs significantly from Chaucer's other ventures in that form, being intended to play the clearly delimited role of prelude to a series of stories. Perhaps for this reason, the Prologue supplies less grist for the critical mill, fewer interpretive problems, and consequently less inducement to hermeneutic virtuosity than the other dream visions offer. Until fairly recently the principal attrac-

---

1. For an assessment of the problematic place of the *Legend* in the Chaucer canon see John H. Fisher, *"The Legend of Good Women,"* in *Companion to Chaucer Studies,* ed. Beryl Rowland, rev. ed. (New York: Oxford Univ. Press, 1979), pp. 464–76. The absence of an essay on the *LGW* from the original edition of the *Companion* (1968) in itself illustrates the problematic status of this work.

tions of the Prologue for the commentators have been extra-literary. Its internal references to Chaucer's earlier works have provoked interest in the poet's life and the progress of his career as a court poet. The textual problems raised by the two versions of the poem have also received considerable attention, which has led to some aesthetic observations, mainly that the F version is more warm and personal than the more tidily organized G version.[2] But on the whole, with some notable exceptions that we shall consider presently, criticism of the Prologue has been tangential, lacking the depth and detail elicited by the other dream visions.

Robert Frank stresses the widely disregarded subordination of the Prologue to the total (though incomplete) *Legend of Good Women.* He allows that the Prologue has "some of the qualities of an aesthetic entity" but implies that it does not achieve high status as an independent poem.[3] Lisa Kiser also views the Prologue in conjunction with the *Legend* and accords it more artistic significance than Frank does.[4] The most influential and sympathetic student of the Prologue, Robert Payne, treats it as an independent work, as do most commentators, and invests it with considerable theoretical importance.[5]

Payne places the Prologue at the heart of his important study of the medieval tradition of rhetorical poetics. He reads the Prologue as a record of Chaucer's struggle to come to terms with his art and with his role as a poet. The poem presents us with "a statement of a complex problem in the persuasive adjustment of language to truth, and several suggestions about the moral limitations which make the problem even more complicated in practice than it is in theory" (p. 111).

2. See, for example, Bertrand H. Bronson, *In Search of Chaucer* (Toronto: Univ. of Toronto Press, 1960), p. 52: "The change in temperature from F . . . to G is from *caldo* to *freddo,* and cannot but strike every reader sensitive to climatic conditions." See also Fisher, *"The Legend of Good Women,"* p. 467.

3. Robert W. Frank, Jr., *Chaucer and the "Legend of Good Women"* (Cambridge: Harvard Univ. Press, 1972), pp. 1–36.

4. Lisa J. Kiser, *Telling Classical Tales: Chaucer and the "Legend of Good Women"* (Ithaca, N.Y.: Cornell Univ. Press, 1983).

5. Robert O. Payne, *The Key of Remembrance: A Study of Chaucer's Poetics* (New Haven, Conn.: Yale Univ. Press, 1963).

Reading the Prologue as a "discussion" or an "argument," in which Chaucer "makes the most direct, complex, and extensive effort anywhere in his poetry to confront and resolve a problem which had occurred . . . in every one of his previous works" (p. 103), Payne is concerned primarily with what he understands the poem to be about. While I admire and agree with much of his interpretation, I find the Prologue itself to be less weighty and substantial than his interpretation of it. His inclination to extrapolate theoretical problems leaves the poem less than fully analyzed and perhaps more than fittingly eulogized. We shall consider Payne's views and Kiser's as well more fully later on.

Robert Burlin's argument for the seriousness, the poetic excellence, and above all the imaginative coherence of the Prologue provides an interesting example of thoughtful interpretation proceeding from questionable presuppositions.[6] Those who have followed my discussion of the unity question in the preceding chapter will understand the grounds for my skepticism about an interpretation that presses the diverse elements of the Prologue into the concentrated form of a spiritual epiphany. Although Burlin recognizes that the Prologue is "in many ways less complex, less dense than the other dream-visions and is fully taken up by an 'occasion' outside of the works of fiction to follow" (p. 35), he is nevertheless unwilling to grant appearances their due, and he proceeds to seek out signs of a deeper, univalent meaning that he presumes to exist. He discovers the "first clue to Chaucer's strategy" in the "language of religious experience," which he derives from Chaucer's eulogy of old books, whose "exalted diction is then imperceptibly extended to the 'adoration of the daisy'" (pp. 37–38). Expanding this discovered coherence, Burlin finds in the twelve-line passage so often cited for its charm—it begins "She is the clernesse and the verray lyght / That in this derke world me wynt and ledeth" (ll. F 84–85)— an analogy with worship of the Blessed Virgin, whence he

---

6. Robert B. Burlin, *Chaucerian Fiction* (Princeton, N.J.: Princeton Univ. Press, 1977), pp. 33–44.

moves easily into an explication of the Prologue as a series of revelations in the "spiritual progress of the poet," culminating in a visionary fusion of books and nature, those "false dichotomies of the waking world" (pp. 43–44).

It may be true, at least for the F version as Burlin claims, that "for Chaucer the dreamer, the pulling tight of all the symbolic threads has profoundly imagined implications" (p. 41) that culminate in "the revelation of an essential reality, where the mysterious forces inspiring the creative act can be seen face to face" (p. 44). But it is hard to escape the feeling that the symbolic imagination revealed here is not Chaucer's but the critic's—or perhaps Coleridge's or Shelley's. The "coherence and integrity" thus derived from the Prologue would transform Chaucer from the rhetorical poet he was to a romantic visionary.

On the contrary, Chaucer's deletion in the G version of the crucial "She is the clernesse and the verray lyght" passage suggests with at least equal plausibility that for him adapting the idiom of religious adoration to the bizarre and humorous worship of a common daisy (not even a rose) was not an epiphany but an exercise in rhetorical play. Chaucer's wrestling with conflicting ideas about poetry is no doubt one meaning of the Prologue, and Burlin confirms Payne's interpretation on that score. But as I believe we can demonstrate without stretching the text unduly, equally important meanings emerge from the evidence of Chaucer's rhetorical approach to poetic composition.

Lisa Kiser's study undertakes to show how the *Legend* as a whole reconciles the conflicting values of classical and Christian traditions. Her discussion of the Prologue resembles Burlin's in its pursuit of symbolic linkages. Primarily by analogical reasoning she develops an interpretation that merges the daisy, the Virgin Mary, the sun, Alceste, and poetry into a transcendent unity that celebrates poetry's power to bring opposing values together:

> With both physical and linguistic ties to the sun, Chaucer's daisy emerges as a strikingly appropriate model for the poet's

craft. Using this flower's close relationship to "truth," Chaucer dramatically illustrates the nature and function of poetic expression. . . . His daisy performs the same intercessory role in the poetic model that Mary performs in the theological one. She intercedes on behalf of humans in the face of God; the daisy intercedes on behalf of viewers in the face of the sun. Even more specifically, both Mary and the daisy have connections with sunlight; like the daisy, Mary was seen as a gentle conveyor of sunlight to earth, for she hid within her the bright sun that was Christ. . . . Both Mary and metaphor, then, are links between earth and heaven. Both intercede on behalf of fallen humanity—Mary in the theological hierarchy, the daisy (and later its personification Alceste) in the secular, poetic one.

(pp. 46–48)

Using medieval methods of etymology and exegetics, Kiser is working *through* the text toward a formulable proposition that Chaucer presumably would have stated explicitly had he not been writing a poem about it. Symbolic interpretation of this kind can tell us something about the ideological content of the poem's language (and also something about the theistic presuppositions of Christian exegetes and etymologists who practiced this method in the Middle Ages), but it appears likely in the present instance that the critic is claiming more than the poem's language bears. The daisy, for example, unlike the rose, the lily, the iris, and several more obscure flowers, carries no traditional symbolic associations,[7] and its supposed significance depends more on the critic's intellectual ingenuity than its own symbolic power. But regardless of the question of plausibility in the interpretation of individual terms, the critic's motivating assumption—that Chaucer encoded in his poem a synthesis and resolution of all these contradictory ideas—eventuates in a highly intellectualized formulation that sits awkwardly on the rocky aesthetic shoals of the poem. From the standpoint of poetics these recalcitrant verbal surfaces are as important as inferred or referential meanings. If we place greater trust in appearances—in what

7. George Ferguson, *Signs and Symbols in Christian Art* (London: Oxford Univ. Press, 1961), pp. 27–40.

the poem plainly says, however inconsistent and self-contra-dictory—and exercise more restraint in inferring concealed univocal meanings, however subtle and complex, we improve the likelihood of identifying Chaucer's operative principles of literary composition, principles that will be embodied in the aesthetic order but may or may not accord with stated or im-plied meanings in particular instances.

As I emphasized in the preceding chapter, the reader who moves too quickly from the contrasts and dichotomies of the text to a supposed unitary meaning excludes too much of Chaucer's artistry. Chaucer's range was encyclopedic, but al-though he shared this bent with the Schoolmen, he was not a theologian or a philosopher. Except for those rare occasions when he faced his God directly—as in the ending of *Troilus* and in the Retraction—the truths he expressed were dis-tinctly contingent and occasional. He maintained an extraor-dinary poetic objectivity (and enthusiasm) toward the con-flicting claims of the world's diversity of things, ideas, and literary forms and styles.

When we speak of Chaucer's self-consciousness about his art and himself—Chaucer was, as we have repeatedly ob-served, a highly self-conscious poet—it is important to differ-entiate between the theoretical generalization and the particu-larity of varying forms and degrees of self-reflexiveness in different poetic contexts. Some of the most thoughtful com-mentary on the Prologue to the *Legend* has interpreted the poem's treatment of the dichotomy between authority and ex-perience—or old books and present natural experience by way of daisy worship—as an important expression of the poet's malaise about himself and his art, but as I think I will be able to show, the poem does not proceed as far as the critics do toward resolving or even defining this issue. In this poem Chaucer really is enchanted with old books *and* with new learning *and* (to some ambiguous extent) with floral beauty. The dichotomy between old books and the daisy is a low-key matter in this poem, unlike Chaucer's treatment of the the-matic possibilities of books/authority versus experience in other contexts, as we have noted before and will have occasion to note again.

If we look at the Prologue analytically rather than hermeneutically, suspending, at least initially, such subsumptive interpretive hypotheses as its major critics have posited, we see a text composed in much the same manner as the earlier dream visions but notably less digressive and irregular and more of a piece. But although it is comparatively more coherent than the others, the result nevertheless is not a univalent poem but only a less complex one. The Prologue is a series of more or less self-contained rhetorical sections strung like beads on the thin plot line of the protagonist's dream adventure. The beads are more uniformly sized and shaped than those in the *House of Fame*, and their hues span a narrower spectrum, but within its limited range the Prologue still observes the integrity of individual structural parts and therefore conveys a multiplicity of "meanings"; it is not univalent but multivalent.

The plot of the Prologue is more purposeful and less elusive than the plots of the other dream visions, and the protagonist is more clearly identified. He is in fact stated to be the author of numerous poems known to be the work of the real Geoffrey Chaucer. In contrast, the protagonist of the *House of Fame*, though called "Geffrey" by the patronizing Eagle, is a humble and conscientious but apparently unpublished hack, seeking "tidings" of love and life. In the *Book of the Duchess* and the *Parlement of Foules* the dreamer is not a writer in the public sense at all, and his mission simply to record a personal dream is correspondingly more vaguely defined. Chaucer's comparatively straightforward self-identification in the Prologue is unusual and will have a bearing in our appraisal later on of the aesthetic effect of this poem's self-reflexiveness.

The purpose of the Prologue being to introduce the *Legend*, Chaucer adopts as his plot the device of dramatizing allegorically the occasion of his commission to undertake that task. The approach to this central matter is indirect, which is to say it entails considerable rhetorical prolixity. Roughly half the poem elapses (more in F, less in G) before the poet encounters the God of Love, who with his Queen will impose the poet's penance and thus shape the plot and provide the cue for the stories. The encounter does not occur until the narrator is about one hundred lines into his dream. Plainly the pace is slow as the poem dilates on such subjects as books, flowers, birds, and love before settling into its central matter.

Like the other dream visions, the Prologue ranges through a variety of literary forms and styles that we can conveniently, though rather loosely, call expository, descriptive, lyric, and dramatic. But the variety is less extensive in the Prologue than in the earlier works. Notably absent is a narrative comparable to the story of Ceyx and Alcione or Aeneas and Dido. Perfectly understandable though it is in a work designed to introduce a series of stories, the absence of a narrative excursus nevertheless contributes to a relatively more even texture here than in the other dream visions, where the mixture of forms and styles produces considerable dissonance. In neither the F version nor the even more restrained G does the Prologue move far from the tonic key. The result is not a different kind of poem but a less challenging one. Like the other dream visions, the Prologue is a poem of surfaces, artfully managed and elegant, but because of its narrower range it is more emphatically and unequivocally superficial.

The poem opens on a ubiquitous Chaucerian theme. This passage in praise of "olde appreved stories" is memorable for its tone and accents of unfeigned eulogy:

> A thousand tymes have I herd men telle
> That ther ys joy in hevene and peyne in helle,
> And I acorde wel that it ys so;
> But, natheles, yet wot I wel also
> That ther nis noon dwellyng in this contree,
> That eyther hath in hevene or helle ybe,
> Ne may of hit noon other weyes witen,
> But as he hath herd seyd, or founde it writen;
> For by assay ther may no man it preve.
> . . . .
> Than mote we to bokes that we fynde,
> Thurgh whiche that olde thinges ben in mynde,
> And to the doctrine of these olde wyse,

Yeve credence, in every skylful wise,
That tellen of these olde appreved stories
Of holynesse, of regnes, of victories,
Of love, of hate, of other sondry thynges,
Of whiche I may not maken rehersynges.
And yf that olde bokes were aweye,
Yloren were of remembrannce the keye.
Wel ought us thanne honouren and beleve
These bokes, there we han noon other preve.

                                                      (F 1–28)

Suspending for the moment the question of relevance to the poet's (later) stated purpose to "speke wel of love," we observe that this tribute to the recorded wisdom of the past is followed by a tribute to the romantic levity of the present. Here we find that the language takes on a different but equally familiar Chaucerian tone. Chaucer's praise of the daisy is comic, ironic, and extravagant:

That blisful sighte softneth al my sorwe,
So glad am I, whan that I have presence
Of it, to doon it alle reverence,
As she that is of alle floures flour,
Fulfilled of al vertu and honour,
And evere ilyke faire, and fressh of hewe;
And I love it, and ever ylike newe,
And evere shal, til that myn herte dye.
Al swere I nat, of this I wol nat lye;
Ther loved no wight hotter in his lyve.
And whan that hit ys eve, I renne blyve,
As sone as evere the sonne gynneth weste,
To seen this flour, how it wol go to reste,
For fere of nyght, so hateth she derknesse.

                                                      (F 50–63)

This passage is reduced and toned down in the G text (ll. G 54–57), and the extravagant rhapsody to the daisy a few lines later as "the clernesse and the verray lyght" (ll. F 84–96)—which is important to Burlin's spiritual interpretation, as noted earlier—is excised altogether. Whether or not this editing was externally motivated, it seems safe to conjecture that it had something to do with the reception at court of a poem commissioned to honor "goode wymmen." To those less ambivalent than Chaucer in their devotion to the courtly God of Love this extended eulogy of the common daisy, religious over- tones and all, might well have seemed a good way off the mark in the direction of parody. But even in its muted form in the G text the daisy passage presents a problem of relevance and continuity.

As we have seen, critics have been uneasy with the disso- nance between the opening tribute to the ancients and the equally fervent tribute to daisies. The various symbolic inter- pretations proposed to resolve the dissonance have overlooked the aesthetic possibilities, the meaningfulness, of dissonance itself. Burlin, for example, recognizes that the Prologue's open- ing lines "seem to have no relevance to what follows beyond a justification of the speaker's slavish respect for old books,"[8] but he attempts nevertheless to subdue that textual sport and weave it into a unifying exegesis, as we have noted. For Payne and others the juxtaposition of books and daisies suggests the familiar Chaucerian dichotomy of historical authority and im- mediate experience, but in this poem the dichotomy scarcely breaks the surface; it is literally as well as metaphorically su- perficial, by which I mean no pejorative judgment. But even granting some symbolic philosophical weight to the daisy as flowers/nature/experience in counterbalance or opposition to the symbolic weight of old books as authoritative wisdom, we are still hard put to discern much tension between the two poles, nothing comparable, for instance, to the intensity of moral opposition between authority and experience that Chaucer develops in the Wife of Bath's Prologue, nor anything as intensely comic as the play on the same opposition in the Nun's Priest's Tale.

Chaucer does draw a relationship between flowers and love, but he does so in a way that has nothing to do with old books. The connecting element is the "fresshe songes" that lovers sing:

8. Burlin, *Chaucerian Fiction*, p. 37.

And thogh it happen me rehercen eft
That ye han in your fresshe songes sayd,
Forbereth me, and beth nat evele apayd,
Syn that ye see I do yt in the honour
Of love, and eke in service of the flour
Whom that I serve as I have wit or myght.
                    (F 78–83)

Only tendentiously can we link these songs that young lovers sing with the wisdom of old books. The latter as a motivating force exerts very little pressure against what is emerging as the central concern of the Prologue. Plot and subject are plainly established here, as the speaker identifies himself as a practitioner of verse in praise of the flower and in the service of love, literary love, that is, as embodied in refined courtly language. In fact Chaucer is observing a distinction here between "makyng" and "poesye," a distinction that was generally observed among writers of the late Middle Ages, as Glending Olson has demonstrated.[9] If "makyng" was perceived primarily as craftsmanship intended for entertainment and refreshment, and "poesye" as inspired morality and learning, there can be no doubt about which of these two distinct poetics governed Chaucer's understanding of the Prologue. Alceste's charge is not that he shall compose poetry about good women, but that "he shal maken . . . / Of wommen trewe in lovyng al hire lyve" (ll. F 437–38, G 427–28). Earlier in Chaucer's defense, Alceste describes his career to the God of Love:

"The man hath served yow of his kunnynge,
And furthred wel youre lawe in his makynge."
                    (F 412–13, G 398–99)

Of course this is Chaucer characterizing himself through the agency of Alceste. Similarly, in self-designations throughout his works he refers to himself as a "makere," never a "poete,"

---

9. Glending Olson, "Making and Poetry in the Age of Chaucer," *Comparative Literature* 31 (1979): 272–90. See also his "Deschamps' *Art de Dictier* and Chaucer's Literary Environment," *Speculum* 48 (1973): 714–23.

as Olson points out.[10] The Prologue's programmatic purpose to introduce stories of "wommen trewe in lovyng" imparts to this poem the center or controlling force that is lacking in the other dream visions. Possible tension among conflicting subjects and genres tends to dissolve in the "penance" Chaucer is enacting in this poem, but this tendency is by no means complete. The penitential purpose does not absorb the poem's extended opening tribute to the ancients, which remains stubbornly independent, perhaps to remind us of that other tradition, the tradition of "serious" poetics. But Chaucer makes no invidious comparisons and no resolutions. He leaves us with two eulogies to different traditions, delivered in different voices, standing in paratactic relation to each other.

Chaucer returns to the subject of "old books" in a long passage added to the otherwise more concise G text. Superficially, in subject matter, this passage is related to the poem's opening eulogy of old books, but it is so different in tone and style that it might well belong to another poem altogether. The passage, cast in the mouth of the God of Love, begins with a scolding of the author and then takes rhetorical flight in a display of pedantic overkill reminiscent of the Eagle and of Chauntecleer:

> Yis, God wot, sixty bokes olde and newe
> Hast thow thyself, alle ful of storyes grete,
> That bothe Romayns and ek Grekes trete
> Of sundry wemen, which lyf that they ladde,
> And evere an hundred goode ageyn oon badde.
> This knoweth God, and alle clerkes eke,
> That usen swiche materes for to seke.
> What seith Valerye, Titus, or Claudyan?
> What seith Jerome agayns Jovynyan?
> How clene maydenes, and how trewe wyves,
> How stedefaste widewes durynge alle here lyves,
> Telleth Jerome, and that nat of a fewe,

---

10. Olson, "Deschamps' *Art*," p. 713. Kiser, however, is no doubt correct in claiming special status for *Troilus*, which in Chaucer's estimation, at least as implied strongly in the envoi, "was the only work in his corpus that approached the greatness of classical literary achievement," that is, the status of "poesye" (pp. 136–37).

But, I dar seyn, an hundred on a rewe;
That it is pite for to rede, and routhe,
The wo that they endure for here trouthe.
For to hyre love were they so trewe
That, rathere than they wolde take a newe,
They chose to be ded in sondry wyse,
And deiden, as the story wol devyse;
And some were brend, and some were cut the hals,
And some dreynt, for they wolden not be fals.
. . . .
What seyth also the epistel of Ovyde
Of trewe wyves and of here labour?
What Vincent in his Estoryal Myrour?
Ek al the world of autours maystow here,
Cristene and hethene, trete .of swich matere.

(G 273–309)

This complex mixture of stylistic verve and self-parodying
pedantry sorts uneasily with the solemnity and philosophical
ripeness of the earlier passage on the old books topos. Yet
Chaucer saw fit, at least in one version of his poem, to include
both, and to extend, at least to that degree, the tonal range of
the poem. The structural ambivalence of the G passage is re-
flected in the commentary on it, some critics, as Robinson
notes, regarding the passage as digressive, others considering
it germane to the argument. In both of these set pieces on
the subject of old books the focus of interest is local and immediate, not global. They exemplify Chaucer's discontinuous
mode of composition. Even in the low-key, thematically and
stylistically constrained mode of this poem Chaucer presents
a sequence of digressive set pieces and occasional stylistic
and parodic extravagances.

The most prolix digression in the Prologue is the discourse
on lordship (ll. F 341–408, G 317–94). In this passage Queen
Alceste, interceding in the poet's defense against the God of
Love's angry accusations, asserts her benevolent influence:

"God, ryght of youre curtesye,
Ye moten herken yf he can replye
Agayns al this that ye have to him meved."

(F 342–44)

The passage remains close to the issue for another thirty lines, referring to the poet's mental and literary limitations but also to his good intentions, before veering into a conventional, impersonal disquisition on the duties of kingship (ll. F 373–408), concluding with the admonition that it is a false sovereignty for a lord to condemn a man without allowing him a hearing, for which reason "oght a god, by short avysement, / Consydre hys owne honour and his trespas."

Compared with the Eagle's excursus in the *House of Fame* or the summary of the *Somnium Scipionis* in the *Parlement of Foules,* the discourse on kingship is a minor occasion. It is also less "digressive," secular kingship being in some sense analogous to the kingship of Love. Chaucer derives some humor from this parodic analogy, and although the discourse on kingship achieves a degree of structural autonomy in the form and style of a conventional admonition to the ruler, it is not notably arresting, nor is it as engagingly outrageous as the Eagle's inflated discourse or as humorous as Pertelote on dreams or as provocative as Troilus on predestination, to mention a few similarly intercalated excursions.

The "dramatic" section of the Prologue lends generic and stylistic variety to the work while providing the principal means of advancing the plot and setting up the *Legend.* The poet's face-to-face encounter with the God of Love and the intercession of the Queen on his behalf have attracted considerable interest for their liveliness and for the light they cast on the "historical" Chaucer, author of all those works listed in lines F 417–28 (G 405–18). The dramatic intercourse conducted by the poet, the God of Love, and Queen Alceste, which fulfills the real introductory business of the Prologue, follows on a series of rhetorical variations—expository, descriptive, rhapsodic, pedantic—all more or less concerned with the subjects of books, flowers, and love. As a textual collage the Prologue concludes with this dramatized inquisition of the poet-narrator. The highlighting of the narrator's identity in this section complements the unusual prominence throughout this poem of a vein of narrator self-regard. Chaucer's self-presentation in the Prologue is such that critics have argued from it that the Prologue is significant as a record of Chaucer's struggle both to master his art and to justify it. Whether the Prologue can bear the full weight of this argument seems to me problematic and worth further consideration.

Robert Payne has argued persuasively that the self-reflexiveness of the Prologue represents Chaucer's progress as a love poet from the *Book of the Duchess* through the *Parlement of Foules* and the *House of Fame* to a culmination in the Prologue to the *Legend of Good Women*. Extending his observation to include Chaucer's self-conscious relation not only to his own poetry but to the rhetorical tradition he mines so deeply, Payne notes in the Prologue many echoes of Chaucer's earlier works. Payne's argument is subtle, and in regarding the G Prologue not as an *ars poetica* but as a "miniature comic myth embodying a poet's search for one,"[11] he makes as much of the Prologue as can be made of it as a document but perhaps more than it deserves as a poem. It should be recognized that Payne's argument is largely inferential and directed outward from the text, into the continuum of historical time—Chaucer's own time, the classical and biblical past, and the future—into which poetical works carry the seeds of their speakers and topics and "germinate, grow, bear fruit, and reseed themselves in successive generations of hearer/readers."[12] While this "organic" metaphor aptly expresses the metahistorical context of the Prologue (as of all poetry), it is not directly germane to the compositional facts of the poem itself. As I have been suggesting, the structural parts of the Prologue, though exhibiting less digressive independence than is characteristic

11. Robert O. Payne, "Making His Own Myth: The Prologue to Chaucer's *Legend of Good Women*," *Chaucer Review* 9 (1975): 210. Note also the emphasis on the Prologue's transitional position between *Troilus* and the *Canterbury Tales* in Alfred David, *The Strumpet Muse* (Bloomington: Indiana Univ. Press, 1976), pp. 37–51.

12. Robert O. Payne, "Chaucer's Realization of Himself as Rhetor," in *Medieval Eloquence*, ed. James J. Murphy (Berkeley: Univ. of California Press, 1978), p. 285.

of Chaucer's compositional method, nevertheless display the generic and structural autonomy associated with inorganic form and rhetorical artifice.

The definitive artifice of the Prologue—and Chaucer's ultimate rhetorical device in self-parody—is its narrating voice. In Chaucer's dream visions, this voice always represents the poet in the first person, yet it is always distanced from him to some extent. Its special prominence in the Prologue gives this work a tighter structure than the other dream visions, yet paradoxically it also deprives the poem of the subtle and unpredictable artistry that makes most of Chaucer's other works so enduringly provocative.

The Chaucerian persona in this poem is an artifice insufficiently artificial to achieve the aesthetic distance Chaucer manages so effectively in other contexts. In identifying this voice with himself as the author of the *House of Fame*, the *Book of the Duchess*, the *Parlement of Foules*, and those other works enumerated in lines F 418–28 (G 405–18), Chaucer brings artifice close to biographical truth, closer, certainly, than he brings his persona in the *Book of the Duchess*, and even closer than the daisy worshiper earlier in the Prologue. But of course some distance remains, enforced by the tone and posture of self-parody that is never entirely abandoned in the Prologue. This posture is rarely abandoned anywhere in Chaucer, as we well know to our pleasure. The closing stanzas of *Troilus and Criseyde*, which, like the Retraction I take to define ground zero—Chaucer speaking *in propria persona*—provide the measure of the pervasive presence elsewhere of varying forms and degrees of self-parody.

But because the margin of pretense in the Prologue is so narrow, the parodic effect is diminished. Some of this flavor remains, as in Chaucer's tongue-tied servility before the God of Love and in Alceste's backhanded defense of the accused poet:

> "Al be hit that he kan nat wel endite,
> Yet hath he maked lewed folk delyte
> To serve yow."
>
> (F 414–16)

But in comparison with the self-parody in the other dream visions, or with the apogee of Chaucerian self-parody in *Sir Thopas*, the effect here is minimal. Its relative closeness to the truth of at least certain aspects of Chaucer's life encourages biographical interpretation, especially of the inquisition section. As if to retrieve some "serious" meaning from a poem that probably deserves Alceste's patronizing judgment of its author, critics have tended to overreach. Even Payne's thoughtful reading seems slightly off-center. Although I would agree that Chaucer, a supremely self-conscious poet, was engaged most of his life in quest of an *ars poetica*, I don't think we can regard the Prologue as more than a halfhearted record of that quest. Compared with the profound and moving explorations he conducted in *Troilus*—explorations in history, literary theory, philosophy, morality, and his own mind and spirit—Chaucer was engaged in child's play in the *Legend* and its Prologue. The resolution achieved in the Prologue is of a low order, directed toward local and perhaps, in the narrow sense, personal issues, such as Chaucer's social reputation among ladies of the court. The inquisition section, cleverly conceived and artfully executed, expresses in sophisticated fashion the modest aim of the Prologue—to introduce a series of stories unambiguously favorable to the character and reputation of women. This is Chaucer at play, rejoining in high good humor the ageless contention between the sexes preserved in the classical, Scriptural, and exegetical heritage, which contention he had joined before and would join again, on both sides of the issue. In this instance he is not only parodying himself as an author but satirizing the sexual conflict itself by the act of advocating, under duress and with unremitting single-mindedness over an extended format, a single side of the conflict. Except as satire, such unrelieved polemic, such extended zeal, runs against the multivalent grain of Chaucer's rhetorical artistry. To sustain such a commitment to the extent imposed on him by his interlocutors was plainly too much for Chaucer. The satiric point was made and the inspiration had faded well before he reached legend 9 and exhaustion. In the Prologue we have Chaucer the rhetorical poet, maintaining enough distance to manage his materials, including his persona, to an artful purpose, not Chaucer the Christian poet, plumbing the moral, philosophical, and religious springs of his art. Despite the biographical realities, the perspective is never entirely serious. The legends of love's martyrs may have satisfied the God of Love and Good Queen Alceste, but Chaucer was already moving in other directions.

As a record of Chaucer's effort to come to terms with his art and its relation to past models and present experience, I think the Prologue falls far short of the *House of Fame.* The Prologue's self-consciousness is less problematic, and despite its comic and parodic moments it is less playful. That is to say, the Prologue tends more to talk about questions that the other dream visions, especially the *House of Fame, embody* in their composition. The aesthetic timidity of the Prologue contrasts with the exuberant virtuosity of those earlier works, in which questions about the validity of poetic truth are not only formulated but also artfully explored in the multiplicity of styles, voices, and forms that Chaucer had at his command. The Prologue is more directly concerned with a local instance than a pervasive problem, an instance, that is, of some sociohistorical interest concerning Chaucer's relationship to the court but of comparatively limited aesthetic and philosophical interest. In this poem, as I have tried to show, the flights are few and they hover relatively close to the ground. I think we can only regard the Prologue as a minor occasional poem, serving an artistically narrow and, for Chaucer, uncongenial purpose.

Why Chaucer returned to the Prologue to produce a revised version can never be known with certainty. Partial answers are furnished by the facts of history, which seem to account, for example, for the excision in G of the ostensible reference to Queen Anne (l. F 496). About the possible artistic motivations for reworking parts of the Prologue we can only speculate. By toning down the narrator's daisy worship, by identifying Alceste earlier, by removing the ballade from thin air and placing it in the mouths of the ladies in the love garden, and by providing an awakening from his dream, Chaucer undoubtedly produced a tighter, more coherent poem in the G version. The legends that follow exhibit the same tendency toward stripped-down narrative. Whatever the legends and their Prologue accomplished for Chaucer in the court of love and in the courts of England and France, they were a retrograde step in the development of his art. Robert Frank's book *Chaucer and the Legend of Good Women* argues the opposite thesis, namely that in the *Legend of Good Women* Chaucer *advances* to a new cohesive narrative. But the evidence of such subsequent achievements as the Nun's Priest's Tale and the Merchant's Tale, to name only two, belies any strong Chaucerian affinity for tightly woven narrative. As all his major works demonstrate, those composed before the *Legend of Good Women* as well as after it, Chaucer's aesthetic impulses did not incline toward univalent cohesiveness and concision. Quite to the contrary, his metier was amplification (though he could produce swift, economical narrative when he wanted to) and he was a flamboyant practitioner of the arts of digression, varied repetition, descriptive enumeration, stylistic variation, formal juxtaposition, generic mixture, and many another form of rhetorical virtuosity. Chaucer's skilled and lively play with language, no less than his insights into human nature, distinguishes his art and assures its perennial freshness. There are flashes of these qualities in the Prologue, and I have tried to do them justice, but Chaucer was cultivating an un-Chaucerian restraint in this poem. Fortunately for us he recognized the lapse and went on to conceive and execute a masterpiece of unrestrained rhetorical art.

6

The Poetics of Pilgrimage

The *Canterbury Tales*

Rhetorical analysis has not been prominent among critical approaches to the *Canterbury Tales*. As I observed earlier, Manly's pejorative view of rhetoric affirmed the predominantly realist tone of early modern Chaucer commentary and devalued the artifices of rhetoric.[1] The pursuit of extratextual "meanings" has produced the familiar interpretive conceptions of the *Canterbury Tales* as "human comedy," "roadside drama," and spiritual and ethical allegory. Although the variety of "human" characters and social situations plainly differentiates the "story" of the *Canterbury Tales*, its subject matter or content, from the more abstract and abstruse content of the dream visions, this distinction induces a too easy assessment of Chaucer's artistic development as a progress from "artifice" to "realism." When we analyze the text of the *Canterbury Tales* and Chaucer's "moulding" of his verbal materials, as we shall do in these closing chapters, it becomes apparent that when Chaucer changed his subject matter from dream to pilgrimage, he did not employ a new poetics. The *Canterbury Tales* is another essay in the poetics Chaucer had been cultivating since the *Book of the Duchess*. Both in its preoccupation with theoretical questions of perception and the validity of language and in its narrower concerns about the shape, style, and disposition of the elements of narrative discourse, the *Can-*

---

1. John M. Manly, "Chaucer and the Rhetoricians," in *Chaucer Criticism: The "Canterbury Tales,"* ed. Richard J. Schoeck and Jerome Taylor (Notre Dame, Ind.: Notre Dame Univ. Press, 1960), p. 285 (first published in *Proceedings of the British Academy* 12 [1926]: 95–113).

terbury Tales betrays fundamental affinities with the dream visions.[2] The expanded range of realistic subject matter by no means forecloses Chaucer's interest in the problematics of language.

The voice that protests its fidelity to truth in the General Prologue is that of a pilgrim rather than a dreamer:

> But first I pray yow, of youre curteisye,
> That ye n'arette it nat my vileynye,
> Thogh that I pleynly speke in this mateere,
> To telle yow hir wordes and hir cheere,
> Ne thogh I speke hir wordes proprely.
> For this ye knowen al so wel as I,
> Whoso shal telle a tale after a man,
> He moot reherce as ny as evere he kan
> Everich a word, if it be in his charge,
> Al speke he never so rudeliche and large,
> Or ellis he mot telle his tale untrewe.
>
> (725–35)

But this voice raises, in a more sophisticated way, the same issue raised by the voice that mediates, equally prominently, between audience and content in the *House of Fame:*

> And to this god, that I of rede
> Prey I that he wol me spede
> My sweven for to telle aright.
>
> (77–80)

The subject is the gap between knowing (or imagining) and showing, and the extent of language's power to close that gap. Perennially fascinating to the reflective writer, this subject was never far from Chaucer's artistic consciousness, and it intermittently occupies the textual foreground in the *Canterbury*

---

2. Donald R. Howard has noted that "the design of the General Prologue and of the *Canterbury Tales* was indebted to the French dream-vision" (*The Idea of the Canterbury Tales* [Berkeley: Univ. of California Press, 1976], p. 155). For a suggested correlation between the House of Rumor and the *Canterbury Tales* see John Leyerle, "Chaucer's Windy Eagle," *University of Toronto Quarterly* 40 (1971): 260. Closer to my sense of the compositional significance of the continuity between dream vision and the *Canterbury Tales* are studies by Cunningham and Mann, fully cited below.

Tales as well as in the dream visions. The presentational voice encloses the work, so to speak, in a frame of conscious artifice to remind us, as rhetorical fiction characteristically does, of the margin between composed text and imagined content.

When we view the *Canterbury Tales* as a text rather than a drama, that is, when we flatten it out and regard it as a single narrative composed by one man, we can see that throughout the narrative Chaucer is self-reflexively shaping the ever-shifting relationship between presentational voice and represented content. Whether the first-person pronoun bears the implied designation "Chaucer," as in the frame, or the given name of Knight or Wife or Clerk, the signs of the poet's rhetorical self-consciousness are as apparent as they are in the dream visions and *Troilus:* abrupt transitions, both explicit and otherwise; overt comments about the problems of telling things accurately; discontinuities; digressions; formalized descriptions and inventories; stylized apostrophes; and many another rhetorical artifice. In its emphasis on its own textuality—what Howard terms its "bookness"—the *Canterbury Tales* invites rhetorical analysis. The question is one of poetics, not of drama, and the answers lie in the text, not in reified characters enjoying privileged status outside the text. Only Chaucer enjoys that status.

THE GENERAL PROLOGUE

We begin our compositional analysis of the General Prologue with a look at the protagonist, the basic presentational voice of the pilgrimage narrative. J. V. Cunningham draws a valid comparison between the author-pilgrim of the General Prologue and the author-dreamer of the dream-vision tradition.[3] In both contexts the form is set in motion by such a figure; that the ordered material is realistic in the General Prologue

3. J. V. Cunningham, "The Literary Form of the Prologue to the *Canterbury Tales*," *Modern Philology* 49 (1952): 172–81 (reprinted as "Convention as Structure: The Prologue to the *Canterbury Tales*," in Cunningham, *Tradition and Poetic Structure* [Denver: Alan Swallow, 1960], pp. 69–75).

and allegorical in the conventional dream vision does not affect our perception of the formal order. But when we undertake to measure this figure's presence in the work, we make some surprising discoveries. As we saw in the *Book of the Duchess*, for example, so too in the General Prologue, the protagonist's persona, though vivid and engaging when it occupies the foreground, is developed minimally and almost incidentally as a sustained presence. Chaucer uses this figure primarily as a compositional device to establish the presentational level of the text and to effectuate narrative movement. As he does with the author-dreamer in the *Book of the Duchess*, Chaucer at times embellishes the "I" of the General Prologue with engagingly "human" touches, and criticism has inclined toward personifying these touches into a full-bodied and full-minded character.[4] We have seen how the interpretive impasse over the "character" of the narrator in the *Book of the Duchess* has inflated that figure far beyond its essentially compositional function and superimposed a tight psychological drama on a poem that is essentially a loose configuration of lyric, descriptive, and narrative discourses.

The *Canterbury Tales* is of course an even looser gathering of even more diverse materials, and psychologically oriented interpretation has similarly narrowed our appreciation of the work's literary scope. In a cautionary prologue to analysis of the General Prologue, H. Marshall Leicester has reminded us that in the *Canterbury Tales*, as in any text, "the speaker is created by the text itself as a structure of linguistic relationships" and that "there is nobody there, that there is only the text."[5]

---

4. Opposing interpretations of this figure are associated with E. T. Donaldson's influential article "Chaucer the Pilgrim," *PMLA* 69 (1954): 928–36, and Bertrand H. Bronson's response that nine-tenths of the (subsequent) "rash of talk about Chaucer's *persona* . . . is misguided and palpably mistaken" (*In Search of Chaucer* [Toronto: Univ. of Toronto Press, 1960], p. 26). Both interpretations reify the speaker, one as a naive pilgrim, the other as a sophisticated raconteur, performing ironically.

5. H. Marshall Leicester, Jr., "The Art of Impersonation: A General Prologue to the *Canterbury Tales*," *PMLA* 95 (1980): 217. Although I think Leicester's basic insight is indispensable to an understanding of Chaucer's art, I cannot always concur in his applications of it. Though he rightly reverses the

Realist interpretation, of course, has insisted to the contrary that there *is* somebody there, expressing himself: in the frame this speaker is identified as Chaucer the naive pilgrim (or as an imagined real Chaucer performing ironically); and for each tale there is a similarly reified pilgrim teller. In insisting that there are no such personae there, only the text, Leicester emphasizes the distinction between persona and voice. The distinction is important. While a persona is a fixed entity that generates a priori interpretive expectations, voice is a flexible instrument—infinitely flexible in the hands of a skilled writer—that forms and transforms itself in the ongoing movement of a text. Undue interpretive emphasis on tellers as fixities can cause us to overlook or misread the conspicuous textuality of Chaucer's art. The aim of rhetorical analysis is not to deny characterization but to locate it close to the textual surface and describe it more accurately as a fluctuating textual process than as a fixed illusionary reality. We shall find that while the pilgrims as narrated objects are highly differentiated in the General Prologue, as narrating subjects in the telling of tales they lose much of their individuality and tend to become assimilated in the basic voice of the text, that uniquely expressive voice that we identify as Chaucerian. From this point of view the pilgrims, including the basic pilgrim narrator of the General Prologue and frame, are compositional instrumentalities or artifices rather than fixed, reified characters.

---

realist procedure of reading a tale as substantiation of the personality of a preconceived teller (since the interpreted teller can be perceived only as the product of a text, not the maker of it), he nevertheless appears to assume that there is a teller there: "I want to use the space my principle gives me to argue that the Canterbury tales are individually voiced, and radically so—that each of the tales is primarily an expression of its teller's personality and outlook as embodied in the unfolding 'now' of the telling" (p. 215). Rhetorical analysis, as I attempt to develop it, finds the "now" of the telling to be much *less* differentiated from tale to tale than the highly differentiated portraits in the General Prologue would lead us to expect. In an important article, Barbara Nolan has expanded and qualified Leicester's analysis of the voicing of the General Prologue, identifying three rhetorically distinct voices: a traditional clerical voice, the pilgrim-Chaucer's voice, and the Host's voice ("'A Poet Ther Was': Chaucer's Voices in the General Prologue to *The Canterbury Tales*," PMLA 101 [1986]: 154–69).

The renowned opening lines of the General Prologue illustrate, at the very beginning of the *Canterbury Tales,* the difficulty of "identifying" the presentational voice, a difficulty that
persists throughout the Prologue and increases in complexity
as the *Tales* unfolds. These artful lines, superbly modulated
through an unusual hypotactic syntax that adds to their grace-
ful dignity, afford no suggestion of an artless pilgrim. Only at
line 19, where the text sets out to establish a particular time,
place, and occasion, do we hear the matter-of-fact voice that
Donaldson named "Chaucer the pilgrim." The earnestly objective attitude and the informal inflections that Chaucer used
in the dream visions, avowing, "thus hyt was, thys was my
sweven," reappear in lines that are overtly presentational:

> But natheless, whil I have tyme and space,
> Er that I ferther in this tale pace,
> Me thynketh it acordaunt to resoun
> To telle yow al the condicioun
> Of ech of hem, so as it semed me,
> And whiche they weren, and of what degree,
> And eek in what array that they were inne.
>
> (35–41)

Chaucer draws only the slimmest line of continuity between
the artful "poetic" opening (ll. 1–18) and the artless circumstantial declaration (ll. 19–42). The phrase "in that seson" in
line 19 ("Bifil that in that seson on a day") refers back to the
preceding lines, but the only other formal literary bond between the two passages is textual contiguity. The viewpoint
shifts from third-person to first-person, and the style shifts
accordingly from literary and impersonal to artless and personal. We can fairly say that two different voices emerge from
these two passages. Critical interest in reifying and identifying these voices—especially the "naive" one—has tended to
distract analysis from the ambiguity of the textual situation.

When we turn to the portraits, we find the presentational
voice still to be elusive and the portraits to be in varying ways
illustrative of rhetorical methods of composition. Jill Mann
has established a firm basis for rhetorical analysis of the portraits in her exploration of the literary antecedents of the Gen-

eral Prologue: "Far from drawing new inspiration from real life, Chaucer seems to have been most stimulated by the possibility of exploiting a rich literary tradition"—that of estates satire.[6] In the Knight's portrait, for example, as Mann has pointed out, "the aim is to suggest an ideal knight by associating him with several recognized chivalric virtues" (p. 107). This aim is accomplished in part by the forthright rhetorical procedure of simply piling up moral terms:

> . . . he loved chivalrie,
> Trouthe and honour, fredom and curteisie.
> Ful worthy was he.
>
> (45–47)

The effect is developed further by the enumeration of campaigns on which the Knight has ridden, "no man ferre," eleven specified plus "fiftene" unnamed. Far from being a realistic itinerary, as some commentators have argued, the list of campaigns is a rhetorical device, like similar lists we have noted in the dream visions, which Chaucer uses to enhance a local effect hyperbolically. It has nothing to do with realism or realistic characterization. To the contrary, it counteracts tendencies toward realistic characterization, as instanced in the *Book of the Duchess,* where the ostensibly differentiated characters of dreamer and black knight articulate in the same reduplicative style similarly erudite lists of classical examples. Such instances, including the Knight's portrait, emphasize the textual surface rather than representational depth, and in so doing they direct as much attention to the undepicted maker displaying his eruditon and rhetorical skill as to the depicted character. Though the enumeration of the Knight's campaigns is a form of rhetorical amplification, it also achieves a remarkable economy, as Mann has observed: "In sixteen lines Chaucer not only tells us that the pilgrimage knight is 'worthy' and

6. Jill Mann, *Chaucer and Medieval Estates Satire* (Cambridge: Cambridge Univ. Press, 1973), p. 17.

experienced, but suggests the whole texture and background of a professional way of life" (p. 11).

While we cannot pause to consider every portrait in the General Prologue, we should recognize something of the variety of presentational modes Chaucer employs. Much different from the matter-of-fact, loosely paratactic mode of the Knight's portrait is the subtle and elusive presentation of the Monk. Both Leicester (pp. 219–20) and Mann (pp. 17–37) point out the obliqueness and ambivalence of this presentation and the difficulty of pinning down the speaker's point of view and "character" as well as the precise target of the satire. The Monk attracts both our moral disapproval and our sensuous appreciation. Delicately turned sarcasm is undercut by scarcely muted admiration. In a passage such as the following, careful reading reveals not a coherently characterized speaker refracting the object from a consistent point of view, but a medley of attitudes in a dynamic and unresolved interaction:

> He yaf nat of that text a pulled hen,
> That seith that hunters ben nat hooly men,
> Ne that a monk, when he is recchelees,
> Is likned til a fissh that is waterlees,—
> This is to seyn, a monk out of his cloystre.
> But thilke text heeld he nat worth an oystre;
> And I seyde his opinion was good.
> What sholde he studie and make hymselven wood,
> Upon a book in cloystre alwey to poure,
> Or swynken with his handes, and laboure,
> As Austyn bit? How shal the world be served?
> Lat Austyn have his swynk to hym reserved!
> Therfore he was a prikasour aright.
>
> (177–89)

As Leicester observes of this passage, "it is all in ironic juxtapositions and loaded words whose precise heft is hard to weigh" (p. 220). The speaker's "real" feelings, his final assessment of the Monk, is withheld, and the speaker remains indeterminate. Leicester cites this indeterminacy, this provocativeness of the unexpressed, as a factor contributing to the "reality" of the text, to "the sense that there is somebody there."[7]

But the somebody who is felt to be there is defined by his absence, not his presence. The designation "Chaucer the pilgrim," although it sounds definitive, is too imprecise to account for the ironic twists and nuances we hear in the lines about the Monk cited above. The conspicuous textuality of this passage, with its complex but masterfully controlled hypotactic constructions and its comically resonating aural associations (pulled hen/hooly men, cloystre/oystre), evokes a consciousness that may contain "Chaucer the pilgrim" but is ultimately located, unembodied, outside the text.

The portraits of the Knight and the Monk illustrate the vitality and formal variety that can be conveyed by a skilled and intelligent poet working within a rhetorical poetics. In the General Prologue as a whole Chaucer develops variations on these forms of presentation. The Parson's portrait, for example, resembles the Knight's in its simple paratactic enumeration of virtues, while the Friar's portrait, like the Monk's, expresses mixed attitudes toward its subject in a conspicuously complex and sophisticated syntax. Whereas the nature and variety of the portraits associate the General Prologue with the genre of estates satire, the Prologue as a whole is an aggregate of individually crafted forms, arranged in a simple contiguous order and held together by the framing device of an incipient pilgrimage. Within the loose and porous circumference of the frame, the similarly shifting and unstable presentational voice of the General Prologue will ostensibly narrate the events of a pilgrimage. As a configuration of forms that present diverse character sketches in different styles from shifting points of view, the General Prologue establishes the compositional pat-

---

7. Leicester, "The Art of Impersonation," p. 220. Whereas Leicester locates this sense of reality in the speaker, Mann locates it in the Monk: "We become convinced that he [the Monk] does not exist simply on the level of theoretical moralising ('what he ought to be' set against 'what he is') but on the plane of real existence" (p. 37).

tern for the *Canterbury Tales* as a total poem. It can be regarded as a template or compositional microcosm of the *Tales* as a whole.[8]

THE PARDONER

From a rhetorical and compositional point of view the assignment of narrating roles to a variety of pilgrims does not differentiate the *Canterbury Tales* from the dream visions as decisively as may appear to be the case from a social-realist point of view. As one studies these narrating voices, it becomes increasingly apparent that in the actual telling of stories they shed their nominal "dramatic" identities and merge into that single voice, infinitely flexible and expressive, to be sure, that we recognize as Chaucerian.[9] When I speak of pilgrim characters shedding their identities, I mean those illusionary identities that name and differentiate them in the General Prologue and that some of them develop to a certain "dramatic" extent in the links and prologues. I realize that in speaking of the pilgrims as autonomous agents capable of shedding or developing their existing identities I am employing a realist form of critical discourse. But some such conceptual compromise or critical shorthand is useful and probably inevitable in speaking of literary characters. The distinction I wish to make, which bears repeating, is between what the pilgrims *are* as characters or objects and what "they" or the voices attributed to them *do* as subjects presenting a narrative.

The illusion of personal identity is carried to varying lengths

8. Though I concur in Howard's general estimate of the relation of General Prologue and the tales, I cannot accept without rigorous qualification his assertion that "the General Prologue in a number of ways reveals and imposes principles of unity upon the tales that follow" (*The Idea of the Canterbury Tales*, p. 156). See especially my discussion of "unity" in chap. 4.

9. This point is stated, though not developed, by Judson Boyce Allen and Theresa Anne Moritz: "Ultimately . . . Chaucer is the only speaker in the *Canterbury Tales*; his rhetoric tells it all" (*A Distinction of Stories: The Medieval Unity of Chaucer's Fair Chain of Narratives for Canterbury* [Columbus: Ohio State Univ. Press, 1981], p. 12).

in different instances. In the Wife of Bath, for example, Chaucer created one of the most memorable personalities in Western literature, though it too has its illusionary limits. But even this vivid personality, evocatively sketched in the General Prologue and elaborated in the Wife of Bath's Prologue, quickly dissipates in the telling of the tale of the hapless knight.[10] The various Chaucerian voices and styles in the tale rarely sound the aggressively straightforward earthiness we associate with the Wife of the prologue. For example, the delicately nuanced opening lines of the tale, recalling "th'olde dayes of Kyng Arthour" and the elf-queen's company and archly lamenting their displacement today by "lymytours and . . . hooly freres," bear little relevance to the pragmatic and distinctly antiliterary personality of the putative speaker. The voice we associate with the Wife in fact disappears as the tale is told. The tale presents an aspect of sexual sovereignty, which dominated the Wife's prologue, but it does so in a predominantly neutral, "unimpersonated" voice. The relation with the Wife's prologue is one of loose thematic contiguity rather than tight personal or dramatic integration. As a rhetorical complement to the prologue, the tale represents a different way for Chaucer to deal with the subject of sexual sovereignty, by amplifying it.

The Pardoner is as celebrated a personality as the Wife of Bath, and there is no dearth of appreciative, if often tendentious, interpretation of this fascinating figure. Indeed the argumentative fervor of much of the interpretive commentary attests to the Pardoner's power to enthrall his real readers as fully as his fictional audiences. The few comments I offer here about the compositional structure of the Pardoner's Prologue

10. For a full discussion of the compositional structure of the Wife of Bath's Prologue see my *Chaucer and the Shape of Creation* (Cambridge: Harvard Univ. Press, 1967), chap. 10. I discuss the artifices and rhetorical instability of the Wife's Tale in "The Question of Genre: Five Chaucerian Romances," *Chaucer at Albany*, ed. Rossell Hope Robbins (New York: Burt Franklin, 1975), pp. 77–103. For a recent realist interpretation of the Wife see Mary Carruthers, "The Wife of Bath and the Painting of Lions," *PMLA* 94 (1979): 209–22. My rejoinder to that article appears in Forum, *PMLA* 94 (1979): 950–51.

and Tale are intended not so much to challenge the veri-similitude of the Pardoner as to relate it analytically to Chaucer's presentational artifices.

Chaucer develops an exceptional continuity in characterizing the Pardoner, beginning with the portrait in the General Prologue and sustaining the character in the headlink and through the prologue and the tale. Only the Wife of Bath among the pilgrims approximates such extensive and full-bodied characterization, and the Pardoner's Prologue, though much shorter than the Wife's, displays a comparatively thoroughgoing characterization, whereas hers is largely an aggregate of dissonant arguments, expositions, and narratives. The Pardoner's Tale, however, is more problematic as an expression of the Pardoner's personality than most commentary has allowed since George Kittredge's famous interpretation of "this subtlest piece of character delineation the poet has ever attempted." [11] The Pardoner comes closer than any of the Canterbury pilgrims to fulfilling the ideal of the "dramatic principle" of interpretation, and the verisimilitude of a wily and eloquent scoundrel is indeed compelling. But even in this triumph of realistic illusion Chaucer is still Chaucer and not Hardy or James. Dispassionate analysis of the text reveals a further dimension of Chaucer's artistry—a dimension beyond realism, I would argue—in which Chaucer artfully turns a mixed text to a unified effect. As David Harrington has argued, in an article that anticipates many of my own observations, "the prevalence of rhetorical techniques contributing to the illusion of speed suggests that the Pardoner's occasionally odd behavior is more for the sake of immediate dramatic and aesthetic expressiveness than for psychological realism." [12]

The opening lines of the tale offer no trace of the self-serving, self-aggrandizing Pardoner of the prologue, not even an allusion to his announced theme of avarice:

11. George Lyman Kittredge, "Chaucer's Pardoner," in *Chaucer: Modern Essays in Criticism*, ed. Edward Wagenknecht (New York: Oxford Univ. Press, 1959), p. 124 (first published in *Atlantic Monthly* 72 [1893]: 829–33).

12. David V. Harrington, "Narrative Speed in the *Pardoner's Tale*," *Chaucer Review* 3 (1968–1969): 52.

> In Flaundres whilom was a compaignye
> Of yonge folk that haunteden folye,
> As riot, hasard, stywes, and tavernes,
> Where as with harpes, lutes, and gyternes,
> They daunce and pleyen at dees bothe day and nyght,
> And eten also and drynken over hir myght,
> Thurgh which they doon the devel sacrifise
> Withinne that develes temple, in cursed wise,
> By superfluytee abhomynable.
>
> (463–71)

Though the presentational voice is not morally neutral, its tone is relatively subdued and remains close to its descriptive material and narrative purpose. In other words, the discourse approaches the transparency of a realist text, presenting the story's setting without overshadowing it. But as the description of the tavern proceeds, the moral energy of the presentation increases and finally explodes at line 485:

> And right anon thanne comen tombesteres
> Fetys and smale, and yonge frutesteres,
> Syngeres with harpes, baudes, wafereres,
> Whiche been the verray develes officeres
> To kyndle and blowe the fyr of lecherye,
> That is annexed unto glotonye.
> The hooly writ take I to my witnesse
> That luxurie is in wyn and dronkenesse.
>   Lo, how that dronken Looth, unkyndely,
> Lay by his doghtres two, unwityngly;
> So dronke he was, he nyste what he wroghte.
>
> (477–87)

The much-celebrated swiftness and economy of the Pardoner's Tale is obviously suspended here—very obviously, as the text launches into a digression of almost two hundred lines. The subject is morality; the tone is moral righteousness, expressed with oratorical bravura; and the materials are a collection of biblical commonplaces and exegetical metaphors that are familiar from the rhetoric of preaching. For example:

> Of this matiere, O Paul, wel kanstow trete:
> "Mete unto wombe, and wombe eek unto mete,
> Shal God destroyen bothe," as Paulus seith.

Allas! a foul thyng is it, by my feith,
To seye this word, and fouler is the dede,
Whan man so drynketh of the white and rede
That of his throte he maketh his pryvee,
Thurgh thilke cursed superfluitee.

(521–28)

In describing Chaucer's loose adaptation of sermon materials to this sermon-like performance, Charles Shain has
pointed out that "the method is to accumulate effects, to ring
as many changes as possible. . . . The only method the Pardoner can be described as using is a *mélange* of all the methods."[13] Thus instead of the tight thematic organization of a
medieval sermon, we have a simple paratactic progression, as

And now that I have spoken of glotonye,
Now wol I yow deffenden hasardrye.

(589–90)

A strong voice holds this string of sermonic materials together
and establishes a compelling sense of presence as it assumes
decisive textual predominance over the fiction introduced
earlier. But strong and compelling as this voice is, spellbind-
ing, even, in its eloquence, its zeal, and its easy command
of biblical materials, we must exercise some interpretive restraint in identifying it with a reified personality. Though it
is Chaucer's most extended discourse in sermonic style, the
same fervent accents and vivid metaphorical language are
heard in numerous other contexts, such as the Nun's Priest's
Tale (which we shall consider presently at some length). The
Merchant's Tale, too, displays similar instances of sermon
rhetoric. Even if the Merchant's Tale was originally intended
for a clerical teller, as some commentators believe, three such
instances of similar language could at most be identified with
a professional class rather than an individual personality. But

13. Charles E. Shain, "Pulpit Rhetoric in Three Canterbury Tales," *Modern Language Notes* 70 (1955): 238. On the loose, themeless structure of the
homily section see also Carleton Brown, ed., *The Pardoner's Tale* (Oxford:
Clarendon Press, 1935), pp. xv–xvi.

however we identify the sermonic style in the Pardoner's Tale, it does not establish a presence that is sustained for long. In fact it subsides as suddenly as it erupted.

The introduction of the three rioters is abrupt and un-prepared for. Despite the reference to "Thise riotoures thre of whiche I telle" (l. 661), we have not been told heretofore of any such rioters. The collocation of this resumed story—or is it the beginning of a new story?—with the preceding or-atorical digression exemplifies Chaucer's method of combin-ing rhetorically distinct materials. As Shain has noted, this quiet country tavern is not even the same tumultuous place described before the homiletic digression:

> Thise riotoures thre of whiche I telle,
> Longe erst er prime rong of any belle,
> Were set hem in a taverne for to drynke,
> And as they sat, they herde a belle clynke
> Biforn a cors, was caried to his grave.
>
>   (661–65)

The indefinite article enforces the sense that this tavern is set in a new rhetorical domain. The voice that proceeds to present the story is ostensibly still the Pardoner's, but it speaks in a dramatically different register; it is notable for its inconspicu-ousness, its virtual transparency, in contrast to the oratorical prominence of the preceding digression. Or is the story the digression? Such is the structural ambiguity Chaucer estab-lishes in this tale that the center is difficult to locate with cer-tainty. In any event, when discourse gives way to story, the powerful illusion of a narrating persona abruptly vanishes. In its place we have a story-oriented text. From line 661 to its conclusion at line 894 the story moves with extraordinary di-rectness and economy, and our immersion in it is assured by the absence of a self-aggrandizing presentational voice. The placement of this subdued voice between the oratorical effu-sions that precede and follow it is rhetorically incongruous but nevertheless hauntingly effective.

The quiet conclusion of the story at line 894 is shattered by an explosive multiple apostrophe. The movement from ar-

tistry to histrionics is as abrupt and total as the earlier movement from histrionics to artistry:

> Thus ended been thise homycides two,
> And eek the false empoysonere also.
>   O cursed synne of alle cursednesse!
> O traytours homycide, O wikkednesse!
> O glotonye, luxurie, and hasardrye!
> Thou blasphemour of Crist with vileynye
> And othes grete, of usage and of pride!
> Allas! mankynde, how may it bitide
> That to thy creatour, which that the wroghte,
> And with his precious herte-blood thee boghte,
> Thou art so fals and so unkynde, allas?
>
>   (893–903)

Of course it could be argued, as most commentary does argue, that a single person, especially a skilled preacher, would
easily command such a contrast of verbal styles. But there is
no person here, only a composed text, a text whose colliding
realms of discourse betray a strong authorial consciousness of
language as a compositional medium, a medium that can be
"moulded like the moulding of wax," to recall the *Poetria nova*,
and disposed in an infinite variety of artful ways, as different
narrative moments might require.

In the Pardoner's Tale Chaucer achieves a tour de force of
both morality and poetics by turning the problematic nature
of discourse to the purposes of popular morality. Playing on
his own acute sensitivity to the gap between knowing (or
imagining) and showing, and his awareness of the ambiguous
mediating function of language, Chaucer has cast the Pardoner's Tale into an illustration of the moral paradox that vice
can portray virtue:

> For though myself be a ful vicious man,
> A moral tale yet I yow telle kan.
>
>   (459–60)

Though the Pardoner is more fully realized as a man, "vicious"
or not, than any of the other Canterbury pilgrims, the structural joints of the text that creates him are nevertheless plainly

visible to the analytical eye. In his characterization the dramatic principle of autonomous verisimilitude competes more powerfully with the principle of aggregative composition and dissonant voicings than is the case anywhere else in the *Tales*, yet the portrait is not fully developed and self-consistent. The conclusion of the tale is a characteristically Chaucerian mixture of modes as the text moves from the ending of the plain narrative (l. 894), to the histrionics of multiple apostrophe (ll. 895–903), to the intimate rhetoric of "Now, goode men . . ." (ll. 904–15), to the incongruous break at "And lo, sires, thus I preche. / And Jhesu Crist . . . / So graunte yow his pardoun" (ll. 915–17), to the renewed intimacy and problematic irony of "But, sires, o word forgat I in my tale: / I have relikes and pardoun in my male" (ll. 919–20), to the explosion of the Host's brilliantly vulgar yet problematic indignation (ll. 946–55), and finally to the Pardoner's silence—"This Pardoner answerde nat a word"—and the concluding intercession of the Knight. All of this movement transpires in the space of a mere seventy lines. Chaucer is crafting a mélange of genres and styles, not unlike the earlier sermon-like speech of the Pardoner that Shain described as a mélange of all the preaching methods. The action takes place on the textual surface, which resounds with rhetorical dissonances. Not surprisingly, interpretation has produced volumes of commentary designed to fill in the gaps and harmonize these dissonances.

The critical assumptions and interpretive method for so doing were established by Kittredge's 1893 commentary. It is interesting to see how Kittredge harmonized these dissonances, which he called "blunders," because he started with a presupposition that rhetorical analysis regards as problematic and seeks to describe and understand. Kittredge maintained that his interpretation

> seems not only to be in harmony with all the phenomena, but even to explain some phenomena otherwise inexplicable except as blunders. That a fortuitous collection of blunders should combine to make up a subtle piece of character delineation is not impossible, perhaps, but is hardly what one would expect. Is it not reasonable, then, to accept an interpretation of the

prologue and the tale which brings them into harmony with what we know of Chaucer's exquisite delicacy of portraiture, and wonderful power of dramatically adapting his stories to their tellers . . . ?[14]

Kittredge began with the teller, whose "known" personality, quirky and devious but "unified" because belonging to a person, became the means of resolving the disparities (or blunders) in the text. Almost a hundred years after Kittredge the personality of the Pardoner is still seemingly taken for granted and still evokes vivid and often inspired interpretive commentary.[15] Rhetorical analysis, in contrast, assumes no such extratextual teller. All there is of the Pardoner is what emerges from this turbulent, gap-filled text. This isn't the voice of the Pardoner, to paraphrase John Barth's admonition about another character, this voice *is* the Pardoner, all there is of him.[16] Of course Chaucer's artistry compels this fascination with the Pardoner, and a truly exceptional character he is. But lest a convention of critical discourse harden into a truth of life, we need to be reminded occasionally that the Pardoner is a fiction and as such is subject to inescapable textual constraints, some of which we have noted, that perhaps are more clearly

14. Kittredge, "Chaucer's Pardoner," p. 125.
15. For example, Donald Howard, *The Idea of the Canterbury Tales*, pp. 345, 363:

> If the Pardoner is not drunk, not a dead give-away, and not the modern stereotype of a homosexual, what is he? My answer is that he is a mystery, an enigma—sexually anomalous, hermaphroditic, menacing, contradictory. He has a magnetic power of attraction partly because he is frightening and loathsome. . . .
>
> Since the Pardoner is an ironist, it is in character that, having said "I wol you nat deceive," he should proceed to deceive them. What does it matter? If they only laugh, he can shrug it off as a joke. Yet he thinks little enough of them to suppose (perhaps rightly) that some at least would be taken in; and he is impudent, dares to confront and challenge them to be his dupes.

16. John Barth, *Lost in the Funhouse* (New York: Bantam Books, 1969), p. 127. For a trenchant discussion of literary voice based on this theoretical foundation see Stephen M. Ross, "'Voice' in Narrative Texts: The Example of *As I Lay Dying*," *PMLA* 94 (1979): 300–310.

apparent to cool analysis than to warm interpretation. The text is not all of a piece, and to reduce it to a dramatically consistent "performance" by a presupposed speaker is to misinterpret an art that analysis shows to be complex and expansive, not narrowly reductive. The voices that we hear in disparate sections do not easily coalesce into one "personality"—not without considerable interpretive effort to "correct" Chaucerian "blunders." More than any of the other Canterbury pilgrims, the Pardoner encourages the realist assumption that the pilgrims are "alive" and existentially distinct from the tales they tell. But like all Chaucer's narrators the Pardoner is a textual construct, no more "alive" than the rioters of his story. The extent to which the Pardoner lives is measured from moment to textual moment, but the cohesion, though remarkable, is far from complete because Chaucer was interested in more than characterization. If the Pardoner is not fully "alive," the text is. Its surface crackles with living energy.

THE NUN'S PRIEST'S TALE

Unlike the Pardoner, the Nun's Priest is a shadowy figure, only a passing designation in the General Prologue, and in the prologue to the Nun's Priest's Tale the Priest speaks only two banal lines:

> "Yis, sir . . . yis, Hoost, so moot I go,
> But I be myrie, ywis, I wol be blamed."
> (ll. 2816–17)

And he is described not at all, though his horse rates a line of description. Lacking a speaker as fully developed as the Pardoner, the Nun's Priest's Tale offers less inducement to critical psychologizing and less distraction from analysis of the textual surface of the tale. Despite the absence of a "known" teller, the tale is told. It is told, as we shall see, by a farrago of voices that Chaucer found suitable, if not necessary, for the multiplicity of subjects, situations, and perspectives that constitute this multifarious work. The Nun's Priest's Tale is a quodlibet of materials in which Chaucer exploits to the point of parody the structural conventions of his art. In Chaucer's poetics, as we have seen from the *Book of the Duchess* and the *House of Fame* onward, the principle of encyclopedic inclusiveness overrides considerations of inner, organic cohesion, and in the comparatively narrow compass of this tale Chaucer tests the limits of compositional coherence. As every reader knows, this short tale fairly explodes with rhetorical energy.

If the end is every tale's strength, a number of recent books on Chaucer have derived their strength from the Nun's Priest's Tale. Following Muscatine's lead, Knight, David, Burlin, Fyler, and Allen and Moritz have accorded pride of culminating place to this tale.[17] All attest to its value as the measure of Chaucer's artistry. "Here, properly more than anywhere else in Chaucer's work," say Allen and Moritz, "the full dimensions of his art come into focus" (p. 220). Critical consensus in this matter is a clear, if not always explicit, acknowledgment of the prominence of rhetoric in Chaucer's poetics, for the Nun's Priest's Tale is both a tribute to school rhetoric (if we can regard its parodic reference to Geoffrey of Vinsauf as tribute) and an exemplary demonstration of the capacity of a rhetorical poetics to generate aesthetic experience—in the form of instructive pleasure—of the highest order. Although rhetoric is everywhere in Chaucer, its presence in the *Canterbury Tales* is nowhere more overt than in the Nun's Priest's Tale; nowhere else is it so obviously, so variously, and so lovingly exploited for artistic purposes.

In the complexity of the Nun's Priest's Tale Chaucer displays, as Stephen Knight has stated, a "highly aware intelligence and assured reference to practically every literary genre

17. "The *Nun's Priest's Tale* not only epitomizes the *Canterbury Tales;* it fittingly serves to cap all of Chaucer's poetry. And so I put it last," states Charles Muscatine, *Chaucer and the French Tradition* (Berkeley: Univ. of California Press, 1957), p. 238. See also Stephen Knight, *Ryming craftily: Meaning in Chaucer's Poetry* (Sydney: Angus and Robertson, 1973), pp. 206–35; Alfred David, *The Strumpet Muse* (Bloomington: Indiana Univ. Press, 1976), pp. 223–31; Robert B. Burlin, *Chaucerian Fiction* (Princeton, N.J.: Princeton Univ. Press, 1977), pp. 228–34; John M. Fyler, *Chaucer and Ovid* (New Haven, Conn.: Yale Univ. Press, 1979), pp. 148–63; Allen and Moritz, *A Distinction of Stories*, pp. 219–26.

in medieval England" (p. 208). Its command of forms is indeed encyclopedic, and because it is composed of so many modes of discourse, it is a tale whose center is hard to locate, shifting as it does among different rhetorical domains.[18] The naturalistic world of the widow's barnyard, rendered in a plain narrative style, sets the narrative base of the tale, or seems to. But the base is scarcely established before it is displaced, subtly but decisively, as the description of a barnyard chicken expands intó the multifaceted anthropomorphism of Chauntecleer. Thus Chaucer superimposes one rhetorical world on another, the intricately stylized narrative of "this gentil cok" and his "faire damoysele Pertelote" upon the plain narrative of the "povre wydwe." On this unstable base Chaucer balances and unbalances style after style, world after world, in a dizzying feat of rhetorical jugglery. Jostling one another and alternating into prominence are the discourse worlds of courtly romance, dream theory, physiological catalogue, narrative exemplum, beast fable, classical tale, philosophical disputation, and antifeminist lore, all punctuated with countless allusions to the ever-conflicting classical and Scriptural authorities, and all filtered through manifold gradations of irony. To drop upon this turbulent mixture the Pauline dictum "al that writen is, / To oure doctrine it is ywrite" (ll. 3442–44) is surely the ultimate Chaucerian jest. "Taketh the moralite," we "goode men" are told (l. 3441) as we struggle (surely not too strenuously) to sort through the daunting array of options. No doubt one of the meanings, or "moralities," of the tale is the futility of seeking fixed meanings, even in authoritative texts. Thus Alfred David finds the main target of Chaucer's satire here to be "precisely the tendency to look for a moral everywhere," a notable futility in this tale that "deliberately lays snares for exegetes of all kinds, political or patristic" (p. 229). Similarly, Stephen Manning sees Chaucer

18. On the tale's shifting perspectives see Fyler, *Chaucer and Ovid*, pp. 158–60. See also Knight's detailed analysis of the tale's controlled variations of style (*ryming craftily*, pp. 206–35).

"poking fun at those who felt that a poem had to have some moral in order to justify its existence."[19] But Chaucer's joke has its serious implications in a question that has profoundly concerned him since the *House of Fame*. Late in his career, at the height of his achievement and reputation, he is still puzzling over the place and validity of language in human experience.

To return to the question of voice and ask who is talking here, the answer can only be multiple. Each of the many realms of discourse that collide in this extraordinary compositional mix has a voice of its own. The Nun's Priest's Tale illustrates in vivid form an ongoing, irregular displacement of presentational voice, on the same structural principle we have observed in the Pardoner's Tale and the General Prologue and throughout the dream visions. Rather than attempt a serial analysis of the entire tale, we can discern the scope of the tale and its principles of composition by plunging into the midst and working our way out through the complexity of Chaucer's narrative polyphony.

Chauntecleer's massive response to Pertelote's homely advice about dreams, in which he marshals all the authoritative evidence at his command to prove his wife (or paramour) wrong, is the kind of rhetorical overkill, flamboyantly digressive, that we have seen in numerous instances in the dream visions. This is Chaucer in coloratura form, producing in Chauntecleer's extended declamation a wonderfully comic satire on domestic relations and male pomposity and pride, which satire in turn is absorbed in the larger literary satire, in the fabular context of manlike chickens. But the root of the comedy is the rhetorical form of the passage. What begins as a retort, delivered by an embodied speaker whose voice harmonizes with his role, quickly slips into a narration, signaled by "whilom," and proceeds to present the first of several narrative exempla:

19. Stephen Manning, "The Nun's Priest's Morality and the Medieval Attitude toward Fables," *JEGP* 59 (1960): 416.

> Ther nedeth make of this noon argument;
> The verray preeve sheweth it in dede.
>   Oon of the gretteste auctour that men rede
> Seith thus: that whilom two felawes wente
> On pilgrimage. . . .
>
> (2982–86)

The story fixes our attention and grows rapidly into a full-bodied and technically complex narrative, with a fully realized setting, major and minor characters, foreground and background, and trenchant dialogue. We become engrossed in the adventures of these "two felawes" as they are forced to part company in their quest for shelter in a crowded and unfamiliar town. Time and movement are precisely rendered as one fellow arises after dreaming of his friend's murder and goes off to his friend's hostelry, only to be told by the hosteler, "Sire, your felawe is agon. / As soone as day he wente out of the toun" (ll. 3030–31). His suspicions aroused, the fellow proceeds, as foretold in his dreams, to the west gate of the town and there discovers the dung cart. His enraged outcry attracts "the peple," who turn over the cart and there discover the dead man "that mordred was al newe."

Thus ends the tale (though its explication is still to come). What a distance this fiction has carried us from the personality of Chauntecleer and his intellectual encounter with Pertelote! Chaucer has shifted presentational voices and situated us in a different realm of discourse altogether. The story of the two fellows is told not in Chauntecleer's recognizably pedantic and patronizing voice but in the unostentatious, almost neutral voice Chaucer reserves for telling stories. This is the voice that narrates the Pardoner's exemplum of the three rioters, the voice of pure Chaucerian narrative, supple, precise, and economical of means. As in the Pardoner's Tale, similarly here the unostentatious narrative voice appears abruptly in the text and quietly establishes its domain. And as in the Pardoner's Tale, when its narrative is completed, it is succeeded by ambiguity and clamor. Between the conclusion of the story and the reasserted voice of Chauntecleer, another voice rises in impassioned apostrophe. I quote from the ending of the story to illustrate the contrast in vocal registers:

> And in the myddel of the dong they founde
> The dede man, that mordred was al newe.
>   O blisful God, that art so just and trewe,
> Lo, how that thou biwreyest mordre alway!
> Mordre wol out, that se we day by day.
> Mordre is so wlatsom and abhomynable
> To God, that is so just and resonable,
> That he ne wol nat suffre it heled be,
> Though it abyde a yeer, or two, or thre.
> Mordre wol out, this my conclusioun.
>   (3048–57)

These chest tones of righteousness are delivered in the voice of pulpit oratory, again reminiscent of the Pardoner's Tale. This is a staple in Chaucer's repertoire, a voice he deploys in variously ironic ways, as in the Pardoner's Tale and the Merchant's Tale, and in unironic ways too, as in the Man of Law's Tale. In the present instance the sounding of the oratorical voice produces complex effects of surprise, ambiguity, and humor. While "Mordre wol out" triumphantly explicates the exemplum, or part of it, this is not *Chauntecleer's* "conclusioun." His explication is articulated in the single flatly delivered line "Heere may men seen that dremes been to drede" (l. 3063). In this collision of voices Chaucer orchestrates a verbal comedy of disproportion and unresolved dissonance. Thunderous oratory is juxtaposed with smug pedantry. The moral of the apostrophe is secondary to Chauntecleer's argumentative purpose, yet in tone and volume it overwhelms the limp statement of his "conclusioun." But the irony is itself ironicized, for we cannot be certain that Chauntecleer's one-line conclusion explicates the story more accurately than the eight-line apostrophe does. The story persuades us that murder *will* out and dreams *are* prophetic. But the responsive reader can hardly escape the conclusion that explicated meaning is beside the point. Chaucer is playing with the *idea* of interpretation, displaying its extremes of flatulence and banality.

What matters is the artful play of incompatible voices—the neutral artistry of the exemplum, the overwrought "interpretation," and the underwrought one. The ironies multiply when we attempt to resolve these dissonances into the voice of Chauntecleer, the ostensible speaker throughout this passage. Of course Chauntecleer is the strutting cock of ancient fable, and he is the satiric image of pride, whose "human" traits Chaucer comically elaborates. But Chauntecleer's personality is fragmented among the colliding discourses that Chaucer attributes to him. In the final analysis, Chauntecleer is a useful name, with attributes more substantial than some Chaucerian characters and less substantial than others. But primarily Chauntecleer is an instrument for articulating an ironically mixed and mismatched array of verbal materials.

In this respect Chauntecleer is no different from the other speaking beasts in the tale, and furthermore, to pursue the analytical point, neither is Chauntecleer existentially different from the Nun's Priest. That putative speaker too is a textual construct, a mélange of vocal registers, scarcely distinguishable in range and variety from the figure we have been calling Chauntecleer. When the text foregrounds the Nun's Priest as speaker, we encounter similar collisions of rhetorical domains, the most flamboyant of them in the climax of the cock-and-fox story. The moment of convergence of these two protagonists of the fable is delayed and wonderfully dilated to accommodate one of Chaucer's most dazzling performances. This seventy-nine-line passage (ll. 3187–3266) can be regarded as a marvel of amplification—to digress so far and so wide on the way to a narrative event—or as a marvel of concision—to compress so much into so tight a space. Following an explicit self-reflexive announcement of intention,

> Leve I this Chauntecleer in his pasture,
> And after wol I telle his aventure,

the narrative begins with a familiar opening formula:

> Whan that the month in which the world bigan,
> That highte March, whan God first maked man,

Was compleet, and passed were also,
Syn March bigan, thritty dayes and two,
Bifel that Chauntecleer in al his pryde. . . .

(3187–91)

The opening of the General Prologue comes at once to mind. Indeed the rhetorical pattern is the same: a long subordinate clause of seasonal description preceding the main clause that initiates the action. And although the presentational voice is nominally different, its sound is much the same. In conducting the ensuing presentation, the Nun's Priest proves to be as elusive an identity as the "I" of the General Prologue, for the speaking voice here too breaks up into kaleidoscopic fragments. The illusion of teller is no more stable than the illusion of tale; both are displaced for the rhetorical moment by overt textuality. In its brilliant diversification of styles and presentational attitudes the text defies interpretive identification of a reified, mediating speaker. We can attribute this spasmodic discourse only to the absent, unreified poet. As this passage illustrates, the materials of the beast fable, even as the narrative climax approaches, are less important as story than as cues for rhetorical action, which is to say the focal point of attention is the medium rather than the story. The line "But sodeynly hym fil a sorweful cas," for example, gives rise to a rumination on the way of the world, parodically cast in a rhetorical cliché and rounded off by a jesting tribute to the integrity of authorship:

But sodeynly hym fil a sorweful cas,
For evere the latter ende of joye is wo.
God woot that worldly joye is soone ago;
And if a rethor koude faire endite,
He in a cronycle saufly myghte it write
As for a sovereyn notabilitee.

(3204–9)

This is quickly followed by the earnest asseveration that this story is as true as the story of Lancelot—another jest on the same recurrent and serious Chaucerian concern about the value of literary art. Can this be the voice of a priest? If so, he is a priest who has literary matters on his mind. And like other Chaucerian narrators, such as "Geffrey" in the *House of Fame*, "Chaucer" in *Troilus* and in the General Prologue, the Pardoner, and the Wife of Bath, this one has difficulty sticking to the point and says as much: the line "Now wol I torne agayn to my sentence" (l. 3214) reminds us of his promise twenty-eight lines earlier to relate Chauntecleer's adventure. The seeming artlessness of this self-reflexive moment recalls our attention to the verbal surface of the text and its artful exploitation—not by the Nun's Priest but by the distanced, unreified poet. In counterpoising story and discourse, fiction and fiction making, Chaucer deliberately plays on the inherent discourse ambiguity of narrative (in contrast to the de-emphasis of this aspect of textuality in a nonrhetorical poetics).[20] This is the highly conscious art of artifice, which includes but also transcends the artlessness of illusion and its expectation of the reader's unconscious complicity.

Turning again, then, to the story, we find it bringing the cock and the fox another step closer to climactic convergence, but only a step. Once again the story cues a self-reflexive shift of focus to the circumstances of its presentation: a few lines of narrative ignite a rhetorical fire storm with the exclamatory "O false mordrour":

> And in a bed of wortes stille he [the fox] lay,
> Til it was passed undren of the day,
> Waitynge his tyme on Chauntecleer to falle,
> As gladly doon thise homycides alle
> That in await liggen to mordre men.
> O false mordrour, lurkynge in thy den!
> O newe Scariot, newe Genylon,
> False dissymulour, o Greek Synon,
> That broghtest Troye al outrely to sorwe!
> O Chauntecleer, acursed be that morwe
> That thou into that yerd flaugh fro the bemes!

---

20. For a meticulous analysis of the components and possible variants of the basic dichotomy of narrator's discourse and characters' discourse see Lubomír Doležel, *Narrative Modes in Czech Literature* (Toronto: Univ. of Toronto Press, 1973).

Thou were ful wel ywarned by thy dremes
That thilke day was perilous to thee;
But what that God forwoot moot nedes bee,
After the opinioun of certein clerkis.
Witnesse on hym that any parfit clerk is,
That in scole is greet altercacioun
In this mateere, and greet disputisoun,
And hath been of an hundred thousand men.
(3221–39)

The burst of oratorical fervor subsides as suddenly as it began. The lines of bloodless pedantry that follow it produce a
bathetic contrast to the moral passion of that fivefold apostrophe. The abruptness of the transition, or rather the simple
collocation, defies the expectations of representational realism. Only by a forced effort of interpretation could we identify these contiguous segments of unembellished narrative,
emotive apostrophe, and arid pedantry with a reified Nun's
Priest. The rhetorical fallout from that narrative cue continues
as the reference to free will and predestination burgeons into
a mock disputation, complete with learned citations to the authorities. After another fruitless reminder that "My tale is of a
cok, as ye may heere" (l. 3252), the text veers into the woman
question:

Wommennes conseils been ful ofte colde;
Wommannes conseil broghte us first to wo,
And made Adam fro Paradys to go,
Ther as he was ful myrie and wel at ese.
(3256–59)

It is no wonder that this aggregation of voices should produce a mix-up of attribution. The lines

Thise been the cokkes wordes, and nat myne;
I kan noon harm of no womman divyne
(3265–66)

represent a speaker trying to evade responsibility for the antifeminist sentiment uttered a few lines earlier. But there are no
words within grammatical reference distance of "Thise" that
can be attributed to the cock. Whether Chaucer slipped up

here in attributing words to a speaker is a purely academic question, for we recognize as we engage with the text that personification of speakers is a matter of local concern only, depending on where the text is at any given moment. And as we see, the text of this tale of a cock and a fox covers a lot of generic ground, from which emerge a number of different voices.

I shall not take the time to point out in detail how everything we have observed about voicing in the passage preceding the climax of the story is structurally reduplicated at the climax itself. The statement that "the fox stirte up atones, / And by the gargat hente Chauntecleer" (ll. 3334–35) triggers another rhetorical explosion, if possible even more audacious in its digressive trajectory and tonal extravagance. The threefold apostrophe to destiny, Venus, and Geoffrey of Vinsauf— a comically bizarre collocation—is held together by the utterly gratuitous connective of Friday, the day King Richard was slain (according to Geoffrey), Venus's day, and the day, we are told, of Chauntecleer's mishap. From the heights of lamentation the speaker plunges to the bathos of self-reflexive regret that he cannot emulate the eloquence of Geoffrey, "The Friday for to chide" (l. 3351). The remaining ninety lines of the tale embody a bristling collage of epic similes, homely proverbs, another oratorical apostrophe, human dialogue, animal dialogue, self-reflexive authorial discourse, and finally an ambiguous concluding "moralite." The final hundred lines recapitulate within their narrow compass the aggregate of rhetorical materials Chaucer has displayed throughout the tale. Abrupt disjunctions and flagrant incongruities produce an unstable mix of flamboyance, blandness, and banality, each shift of style, subject, and perspective emitting a sudden burst of rhetorical energy or a sudden deflation. A stunning example of the latter occurs when the narrative plummets—in the space of three lines—from the epic simile of the keening wives of Roman senators slain by Nero to the matter-of-fact report of an incident in a barnyard—thus returning the exuberantly errant narrative to the rhetorical level on which it began, but only briefly, before it takes off again, jouncing its way to a conclusion.

The emphasis of the Nun's Priest's Tale on rhetorical variety inevitably depreciates depth of illusion in favor of brilliance of surface. As in self-reflexive narrative in general, the interplay of story and discourse is unbalanced in favor of discourse, but Chaucer manipulates that binary relation in unfailingly interesting and engaging ways. The text is conspicuously surface-oriented, and in our rhetorical analysis we have stressed its linear order and successive displacements of presentational voices. But the tale's complexity and the aesthetic pleasure we derive from it depend on the unique manner in which Chaucer subordinates the tale's vertical structure, or hierarchy of illusions, to its dominant surface. In this tale the disparities among levels of illusion are extreme—a man is the protagonist in a tale told by a chicken, who in turn is the protagonist in a tale told by a man—and this incongruity produces humor as well as illusionary ambiguity and instability.[21] In other instances, as in the Knight's Tale, the easy confusion between the Knight's discourse and Theseus's produces a less explosive effect because the two figures, though occupying distinct levels of illusion, are referentially similar.

Because the Nun's Priest's Tale is an extreme and humorous expression of Chaucer's ambivalent attitude toward the art of illusion making—how true it is and enthralling, and how false and transitory—it illustrates especially well a cautionary critical principle about Chaucerian interpretation in general. Failure to pay due attention to the actualities of compositional structure can result in uncritical immersion in illusion. The predisposition of some critics to "dramatize" the pilgrim tellers by viewing their tales as "speeches" tended to rigidify the

21. The hierarchy of Canterbury stories and tellers is an illusionary phenomenon of infinite possible reach, which we can visualize as follows, starting at an arbitrarily chosen "low" point in the Nun's Priest's Tale and moving "upward" through the entire *Canterbury Tales*: (1) in the exemplum of the "two felawes" the surviving fellow tells the tale of his friend's death to the rulers of the city: "Harrow! allas! heere lith my felawe slayn!" (l. 3045); (2) the fellow becomes himself a tale, told by Chauntecleer; (3) Chauntecleer the teller becomes a tale told by the Nun's Priest; (4) the tale-telling Nun's Priest becomes a tale told by the pilgrim-reporter known to us as "I" and usually designated in criticism "Chaucer the pilgrim"; (5) "Chaucer the pilgrim" becomes a fiction made by Chaucer.

relation of discourse to story. It simplified the tales by regarding them as homogeneous units subordinated to a larger purpose, namely to characterize their tellers. Interpretation proceeding from the "roadside drama" theory either ignored features of the tales that conflicted with consistent characterization of the teller or adjusted irregularities to conform with a complex personality formulated by the interpreter.

Rhetorical analysis is not constrained by the rigid presupposition of a dramatized presence waiting to be discovered and is less inclined to filter and purify or rationalize the text than to embrace it, all of it. As our brief investigation of the Nun's Priest's Tale has suggested, the relation between speaking voice and tale it tells is not constant but variable, frequently shifting and redefining its terms in the course of narration. Speakers who are "low" on the hierarchy, or "internal," function in the same ambiguous way as those who are "higher"; they are dramatized and de-dramatized and re-dramatized from moment to moment. Their status is fundamentally unstable. The tale is not the unified speech of a dramatized character but a sequence of discourses whose presentational voices are always subject to nominal displacement. But whatever their names—Nun's Priest, Chauntecleer, the hosteler—these voices constitute the global Chaucerian voice. This is the universal voice that we rightly identify throughout the canon as Chaucerian, without quotation marks or qualifying epithets such as "the pilgrim" or "the narrator" or even "the man." Such qualifiers obscure the absolute epistemological difference between the absent, unembodied author and the multiplicity of voices that emerge from the text. All of them are "artificial." Only the artificer is real, and that is *because* he is absent and unembodied. In the fundamental binary structure of this text—the relation of discourse to story, or subject to object—the object is always the virtuoso Chaucerian voice. That is what strikes our eye and our ear. The ultimate and only subject is the absent poet. He alone enjoys privileged status outside the language of the text.

7

Endings

The Manciple's Tale is Chaucer's last fiction, the Parson's Tale his last discourse, and the Retraction his valediction, a prayer. This sequence closes Chaucer's career and appears also to resolve his lifelong ambivalence about the nature and efficacy of the writer's art. The Manciple's Tale, the last and the briefest of the completed narratives, is a provocative—perhaps even a desperate—last inquiry into the relation between language and truth, thinly disguised as a fable about the crow. In the Parson's Tale, of course, Chaucer moves out of fiction making altogether, and in the Retraction he explicitly renounces all the works that embody the poetics I have attempted to educe and elucidate in these chapters. For an artist whose métier is artifice and the accommodation of disjunct materials, Chaucer appears to have achieved the ultimate disjunction, the transcendence of artifice. But it is difficult to assess conclusively Chaucer's last words on the subject of his art; no doubt the master of obliquity would not have it otherwise.

THE MANCIPLE'S TALE

The critical fortunes of the Manciple's Tale have been closely bound up with the fortunes of rhetoric. Speaking about Chaucer and rhetoric to a learned audience in 1926, Manly felt it necessary to summarize the plot of this unfamiliar tale; he then proceeded to dismiss the tale, rather contemptuously, for being "padded" with rhetoric and "entirely devoid of life."[1] As I have tried to demonstrate, the discovery of life in

---

1. John M. Manly, "Chaucer and the Rhetoricians," in *Chaucer Criticism: The "Canterbury Tales,"* ed. Richard J. Schoeck and Jerome Taylor (Notre Dame,

a text depends on where one looks. Perhaps at this stage I need not stress that Chaucer's *language* lives, and its points of highest intensity lie on the textual surfaces and along the ever-shifting margins between discourse and story, *récit* and *histoire*.

Manly based his disparagement of the Manciple's Tale on several accurate observations. He observed correctly that more than half of the lines of the tale are "patches of rhetoric," and less than half of the tale is "plot." He also observed correctly, if somewhat recklessly, that "no effort was made by the author to conceive any of his characters as living beings." And finally he observed that "the tale is not particularly appropriate to the Manciple" (p. 284). Such are the wonderful turns of critical understanding that we are now able, in the new light of rediscovered rhetorical values, to convert all these terms of disparagement to terms of praise. In a detailed and sensitive rhetorical analysis Stephen Knight has shown how skillfully Chaucer managed his materials,[2] though he does not pursue the theoretical implications of his analysis. Britton Harwood's thematic interpretation also emphasizes rhetoric in arguing that the subject of the tale is language and the relation between words and things.[3] Donald Howard offers a provocative interpretation in a similar vein and also points out that "the tale is neatly structured on principles of medieval rhetoric."[4] All of these critics advance our understanding of the tale and educe considerably more sympathy for the artistic value of rhetoric than Manly would allow. But none of them regard rhetoric as the foundation of Chaucer's poetics. All fall back finally on the "dramatic" principle and attempt to rationalize and justify the tale either as characteristic of the Manciple

---

Ind.: Notre Dame Univ. Press, 1960), pp. 284–85 (first published in *Proceedings of the British Academy* 12 [1926]: 95–113).

2. Stephen Knight, *ryming craftily: Meaning in Chaucer's Poetry* (Sydney: Angus and Robertson, 1973), pp. 161–83.

3. Britton J. Harwood, "Language and the Real: Chaucer's Manciple," *Chaucer Review* 6 (1972): 268–79.

4. Donald R. Howard, *The Idea of the Canterbury Tales* (Berkeley: Univ. of California Press, 1976), p. 300.

(Harwood and Howard) or as uncharacteristic of him (Knight). The result is interpretations that are plausible, if tendentious, but inevitably partial, in both senses of the word. In reducing and at times constraining the tale into the univocal expression of a reified speaker—whether the Manciple or some other, unspecified, speaker—such interpretations fail to account adequately for the rhetorical fragmentation of the tale. In particular they overlook or undervalue the humor, the serious playfulness, that lies at the root of this tale and expresses Chaucer's ambivalence about language, which differentiates him, as *homo rhetoricus*, from the *homo seriosus* of realist poetics.

John McCall has captured the essential spirit of the Manciple's Tale in his comment on the concluding string of admonitions addressed to "my sone":

> This preachment, like the classical story which gives rise to it and like the whole of the Manciple's performance, tends to comic self-destruction. It teaches its moral [and] belies its moral. . . . With assistance from all over, the Manciple has disclosed a timeless message. Its truth extends all the way from the pagan antiquity of Apollo and the crow . . . through the present time of Flemish proverbs (349) and garrulous mothers, on to the apparently "endelees" reaches of moral contradiction. But the whole thing is not simply a bizarre parody of moralizing; it is really moral in a sense which the Manciple and no other simpleminded preacher could understand. It tells of man's silly, extreme reactions to what is wrong: of tendencies to protest overmuch or inhumanly, or not to protest at all, to be quiet and let things go.[5]

The "self-destruction" of the tale *is* comic in playfully evoking Chaucer's serious and persisting puzzlement over the validity of man's efforts to capture reality with words.

If the Nun's Priest's Tale reaches an extraordinary complexity of acentric structure, we can perhaps see the Manciple's Tale as a simpler example, a lucid paradigm, of the fundamentally ambiguous condition of language. This shortest of the tales and last of the Canterbury series embodies Chaucer's

---

5. John P. McCall, *Chaucer among the Gods: The Poetics of Classical Myth* (University Park, Pa.: Pennsylvania State Univ. Press, 1979), p. 152.

final essay in the art he has practiced and ruminated over since the *Book of the Duchess* and the *House of Fame*. The Manciple's Tale is his ultimate self-conscious fiction.

We begin our analysis with Manly's observation (though not with his presuppositions) that the text is mostly "rhetoric." His count of 61 percent rhetoric to 39 percent story seems inaccurate to me, though the general idea is incontestable. I find the balance more even, with the edge to rhetoric by 128 lines to 126.[6] Obviously the reader who is seriously absorbed in the events in Phebus's household is in for an aggravating and tiresome reading experience as he stumbles through the rhetorical "padding." Even the story itself, as Manly rightly noted of its character descriptions, is highly rhetorical and conventionalized. This is a story of love and death, but certainly not in the grand romantic manner. It is a story deliberately stylized by its author and distanced from "the forms and activities of life," not because Chaucer was indifferent to life or to art but because he was interested in a question larger and more vital than verisimilitude: the question of human perception and the role of language in that vital activity.

The story of Phebus, then, is less important in itself than in its function as an instrumentality in a larger process. The story is not as devoid of life as Manly claimed—it has sufficient substance and generates sufficient interest to test our patience with the many interruptions in its narration. But the story is only part of a text, in which it shares centrality with the digressions that interrupt and almost overwhelm its telling. The center of the text fluctuates between story and storytelling, and it does so in a more overt and sharply differentiated way than the several other acentric narratives we have examined. But the center of our analytical interest is not ambiguous: we are fascinated by Chaucer's handling of his textual surface, on which he brings into high visibility the processes of narrative composition. The prominence of di-

6. My attributions are as follows: Tale: lines 105–47, 155–59, 196–200, 203–4, 238–308; Rhetoric: 148–54, 160–95, 201–2, 205–37, 309–62.

gressive discourse and its substantive equality with story produces a highly concentrated form of self-reflexive narrative, which deliberately exaggerates comic dissonances and incongruities.

Our attention is intermittently but frequently drawn to the textual surface and to the structuring activity of composing it. This occurs most notably in the digressive passages, particularly when the narrating voice speaks about the problems of narrating. A few examples:

> But now to purpos, as I first bigan
> (155)

. . .

> His wyf anon hath for hir lemman sent.
> Hir lemman? Certes, this is knavyssh speche!
> Foryeveth it me, and that I yow biseche.
> (204–6)

. . .

> I am a boystous man, right thus seye I.
> (211)

. . .

> But, for I am a man noght textueel,
> I wol noght telle of textes never a deel;
> I wol go to my tale, as I bigan.
> (235–37)

. . .

> But, as I seyde, I am noght textueel.
> (316)

Such explicitly self-conscious narrating emphasizes discourse at the expense of story, and of course it also strongly implies the presence of a speaker. But before turning to the vexed matter of the Manciple's character and personality I want to consider more fully the tale's stress on surface.

As the passages listed above indicate, the digressive half of the text effects a decisive orientation toward the compositional surface. The ultimate digression, the concluding fifty-line moralization of the story—certainly a tour de force for a teller who is not "textueel"—irresistibly fixes our attention on the presentational surface and consigns fictive Phebus to the far recesses of our consciousness. But even the Phebus story itself is strongly surface-oriented, though this orientation is effected by structural means rather than overt self-reflexiveness. Again, Manly was right about the conventionality of the story's materials, which highlight the "artificial" nature of the narrative. The description of Phebus, for example, is cast in the conventional idiom of romance:

> This Phebus, that was flour of bachilrie,
> As wel in fredom as in chivalrie,
> For his desport, in signe eek of victorie
> Of Phitoun, so as telleth us the storie,
> Was wont to beren in his hand a bowe.
>
> (125–29)

In form too this passage is distinctly fashioned as a rhetorical set piece. Its beginning is signaled by the demonstrative adjective, and its conclusion is indicated internally by completed sense and externally by the new beginning articulated in the line that follows it: "Now hadde this Phebus in his hous a crowe" (l. 130).

Pace Henry James, Chaucer constructs his narrative with such "blocks" of language, and he arranges and exploits these blocks to the rhetorical effects that distance us from the represented life and bring us close to the life of the representer, to his shaping hand and his active mind. The block of composition, or verse paragraph, describing Phebus's crow is followed immediately by one describing his wife. The juxtaposition of the opening lines of these two blocks produces an interesting effect:

> Now hadde this Phebus in his hous a crowe
> (130)
>
>   .   .   .
>
> Now hadde this Phebus in his hous a wyf.
> (139)

In these lines the tension between fiction and rhetoric, between content and medium, is heavily weighted in favor of medium. Repetition is of course a major rhetorical device; that the second line repeats the first exactly, except for one word, produces a rhetorical impact, an intrusion of style between reader and illusion. The words "crowe" and "wyf," occurring in otherwise identical contexts, paratactically related, produce a humorous dissonance that both imaginatively distances and morally diminishes Phebus. Through the rhetorical management of form Chaucer has characterized Phebus as a brainless husband who regards his wife and his pet crow as possessions of equal value. As in the typical fabliau, the stage is set for poetic justice.

In other ways too the Phebus story displays a rhetorical maker at work. Description and dialogue dominate the narrative to the extent that action, like character and setting, plays a perfunctory supporting part. The climactic slaying of the (nameless) wife is dispatched in two lines:

> His bowe he bente, and sette therinne a flo,
> And in his ire his wyf thanne hath he slayn.
> This is th'effect, ther is namoore to sayn.
>
> (264–66)

The real action is language, and it erupts in Phebus's reaction to his deed. His impassioned language resonates in many directions, striking a multitude of wrong or inappropriate notes in a series of assorted exclamations and apostrophes. Phebus condemns the truthful crow for a traitor and eulogizes his guilty wife as innocent:

> "Traitour," quod he, "with tonge of scorpioun,
> Thou hast me broght to my confusioun;
> Allas, that I was wroght! why nere I deed?
> O deere wyf! o gemme of lustiheed!
> That were to me so sad and eek so trewe,
> Now listow deed, with face pale of hewe,
> Ful giltelees, that dorste I swere, ywys!
> O rakel hand, to doon so foule amys!
> O trouble wit, o ire recchelees.
>
> (271–79)

The rhetoric of this passage—it goes on to warn mankind against "rakelness" and concludes, "Allas! for sorwe I wol myselven slee!" (l. 291)—is not without some referential validity as an expression of Phebus's "confusioun" and grief, but this is a finely wrought confusion. The literary effect is larger than the "life" of the character, for it also embraces the medium and illustrates, through the humor of overstatement, misstatement, and irrelevance, the extent to which the character *is* the medium.

From the morally askew world of Phebus's household, in which infidelity is punished by death but eulogized as innocence, in which the truth teller is excoriated and deprived of speech, and in which the murderer is not punished at all, a moral lesson emerges:

> Lordynges, by this ensample I yow preye,
> Beth war, and taketh kep what that ye seye:
> Ne telleth nevere no man in youre lyf
> How that another man hath dight his wyf;
> He wol yow haten mortally, certeyn.
>
> (309–13)

Never tell the truth to a cuckold, for he will hate you mortally—surely a sovereign notability, worthy of inscription in a rhetor's chronicle! The incongruity between the moral and the tale, plus the manifest superficiality of the tale itself, reduces the "meaning" to nonsense but produces a wonderfully artful entertainment. This is an art of subtle artifice and fine discriminations, an art that brings the reader into the process and invites him to recognize the making as well as the make-believe and to appreciate the ambiguous and finally comic interplay between them.

But as in so much of Chaucer, the effect of the Manciple's Tale is not single but multiple. Throughout the tale, inseparable from the comic treatment of compositional artifice, runs a vein of epistemological seriousness. The situation is not unlike that in the *House of Fame,* and indeed Chaucer concludes the Manciple's Tale, his final essay in fictional narrative, with a verbal and thematic echo of that work:

> "My sone, be war, and be noon auctour newe
> Of tidynges, wheither they been false or trewe.

Whereso thou come, amonges hye or lowe,
Kepe wel thy tonge, and thenk upon the crowe."

(359–62)

This conclusion to the Manciple's Tale is also the conclusion to
the lengthiest of its so-called digressions, that aggregate of
discourses that challenges the idea of centrality by displaying
the act of telling as prominently and palpably as the told tale.
That the tale ends within the direct discourse of a "digression" and fails to resolve the issue on the level of the putative
teller's presentational voice leaves us further removed from
both Phebus and the Manciple. The distancing of both story
and teller enhances the textual surface and its author as the
true center of the work. But for an author as self-conscious
and ambivalent about his art as Chaucer was, the truth of textuality is still contingent and problematic.

Here in his last fiction Chaucer is still preoccupied with the
epistemological question he raised directly in the *House of
Fame* and explored obliquely, if not directly, in almost all his
narratives. The "digressions" in the Manciple's Tale—let us
refer to them collectively as discourse in distinction to story—
represent Chaucer's last word, be it ever so ambiguous, on the
matter of language, truth, and the writer/speaker. And what
is the last word on that profoundly troublesome question but
silence, counseled over and over again in the forty-four lines of
maternal advice that bring the narrative to a gregarious and
structurally unstable conclusion. This string of seventeen
proverbs and apothegms produces considerable ironic humor, witness the rhetorical overkill on the subject of restraint
and the twelve repetitions of the phrase of address, "my
sone." The images, too, though largely proverbial, achieve a
comic resonance because Chaucer renders so crisply material
that is sometimes bizarre, such as this motherly advice:

"Wostow wherof a rakel tonge serveth?
Right as a swerd forkutteth and forkerveth
An arm a-two, my deere sone, right so
A tonge kutteth freendshipe al a-two."

(339–42)

And there is more than a touch of comic excess in the metaphor of the mouth as a fortification:

> "My sone, God of his endelees goodnesse
> Walled a tonge with teeth and lippes eke,
> For man sholde hym avyse what he speeke."
> (322–24)

But the superabundance of talk about silence, an amusing paradox in itself, bears a serious meaning. It is a structural reduplication of the contention between story and discourse that shapes the Manciple's Tale as a whole. Brief as the narrative is, the repeated interruptions of the story by digressive discourse give notice of an endless reserve of verbosity. From the first "But now to purpos" (l. 155) we sense an opposing energy of discourse that will not be repressed, and it *is* not. For example, the quiet observation that no one can alter the natural inclinations of God's creatures, apropos women's inconstancy and men's jealousy, looses a small cascade of instances. With a seemingly irresistible momentum, the text surges into the rhetorical domain of natural history (leaving the Phebus fiction far behind), expounding with illustrative detail in successive verse paragraphs the natural lore of birds, cats, and she-wolves. (Never mind that the archly ironic mismoralizing of these examples fails to offset their patent antifeminism; the humor here is beside my present point.) Hardly has the speaker regained the thread of story than the word "lemman" springs another extended discourse, this time on semantics and the connotational vagaries of language, again amply illustrated with homely detail.

This discussion of semantics is notable in many respects, all bearing on Chaucer's continuing interest in the question of language. The passage bursts out of its narrative context at line 205:

> And so bifel, whan Phebus was absent,
> His wyf anon hath for hir lemman sent.
> Hir lemman? Certes, this is a knavyssh speche!
> Foryeveth it me, and that I yow biseche.
> (203–6)

The energetic self-reflexiveness of these lines introduces a "building block" of discourse that is neatly (if abruptly) enclosed thirty-three lines later with the formula "I wol go to my tale, as I began." This speech is cast in the voice of a "boystous man," one at pains to assert that he is "noght textueel," but Chaucer simultaneously blurs this characterization with the plainly "textueel" nature of the speech. It begins with a learned allusion to "The wise Plato," who says, "The word moot nede accorde with the dede" (l. 207), and goes on to build a sophisticated argument for the deceptive nature of language (including a learned but gratuitous citation of Alexander). Language can make us think the thing that is not, can make us think a "lady" different from a "lemman" when in fact there is no difference: "Men leyn that oon as lowe as lith that oother" (l. 222). The point is further enforced, and rhetorically amplified, by a similar comparison of "capitayn" and "outlawe or theef," likewise words that deceive us into believing there is a difference.

Of course this is a loaded and tendentious argument, bearing more than a tinge of proletarian cynicism toward the privileged and the powerful. The message seems to be consistent with other expressions of cynicism, such as the immoral moral of the Phebus story and the lengthy maternal admonition against speech. Yet the exuberance and humor of the tale, the artfully managed overstatements and understatements, the discontinuities, incongruities, and comic ironies counterbalance the cynicism, though they do not erase it. The tale accommodates both.

Thus we come to the question of meaning. As usual, Chaucer clouds the answer in ambiguity, but if we take his ambiguity at face value and resist, at least tentatively, the urge to resolve and "unify," we can arrive at a just estimate of the Manciple's Tale and its special place in the *Canterbury Tales* and indeed in the canon. First of all, as I have been urging throughout these pages, we need to refine the question. It is not simply *what* is the meaning, but *where* is it, and *whose* is it. Most commentary posits the Manciple as the agent of meaning and undertakes to assimilate the tale's diversities and contraditions into his "personality" as we know it from the General Prologue and the Manciple's Prologue. Thus Harwood would interpret the tale as "a covert indictment in which the Manciple sneers at those who can be distracted from empirical reality by language," and he finds it "more characteristic of the Manciple and more unified with his Prologue than has often been thought."[7] Howard dramatizes the attribution more emphatically: "But the Manciple *was* described in the General Prologue. His contretemps with the Cook reminds us of his unsavory character—and makes him more unsavory. And his tale is cynical, destructive. . . . His style is unsavory like the man himself. His tale destroys everything and does it coldly."[8] Knight is not so sure. His close reading reveals passage after passage that "does not sound like the work of the Manciple," that is "too subtle to sound like the Manciple," that comes from a narrator who is "proving to be too learned and also fairly generous with his learning."[9] The "O rakel hand" speech seems "inconsistent from a narrator more noted for crispness than grand passion . . . and seems even more beyond him than what we have noted before" (p. 179). But if the tale does not suit the Manciple, Knight believes that it does suit some other, undesignated, teller: "Overall it implies quite a strong personality in its narrator, though not one that bears any resemblance to the Manciple as we know him" (p. 172).

All of these critics advance our understanding of the Manciple's Tale by increasing our awareness of its rhetorical orientation. But in the end all revert to an extratextual teller—be he the Manciple or not—as the source of meaning. In other words, rhetoric is finally subordinated to drama as critical interpretation shifts from the text to its speaker. Such a reading, apparently based on "dramatic" or psycho-realist presuppositions, finally reduces a multivoiced text to a univocal one. On

---

7. Britton J. Harwood, "Language and the Real: Chaucer's Manciple," p. 268.

    8. Donald R. Howard, *The Idea of the Canterbury Tales*, p. 305.

    9. Stephen Knight, *ryming craftily*, p. 175.

the other hand, if we entertain the rhetorical assumption that Chaucer is more interested in ways of talking—or of simulating talk in writing—than in creating the illusion of psychologically plausible and consistently developed characters, we can account for more of the text's observed features than a realist orientation is able to accommodate. For example, it becomes unnecessary, even misguided, to rationalize a Manciple (or other, undesignated, pilgrim speaker) whose personality is sufficiently capacious to account for both "boystous" and "textueel" sequences. Rather than resort to tendentious conceptualizing of an extratextual persona in whom such contradictory features might seem plausible, as in the roadside drama theory of interpretation, we should accept the text's invitation to appreciate the compositional play of different styles and voices from a variety of literary conventions. Chaucer's poetics opens the Manciple's Tale to a range of subjects and perspectives that are realistically incompatible—the classical and the vulgar, the shrewd and the ingenuous—but that intermingle nevertheless in a unique rhetorical felicity. In style too the Manciple's Tale is not limited even to the opposition of "boystous" and "textueel." Chaucer's expansive poetics allows him scope to orchestrate a spectrum of shadings from bombast to subtle irony.

Another observed feature of the text that seems to be squeezed out in realist interpretation is humor. We have noted Chaucer's play with ironic prolixities, with overstatement and understatement, with the collisions of discordant realms of discourse. The text offers this entire dimension of compositional virtuosity for our delectation. The humor is largely intellectual, depending for its effect on the reader's active consciousness of what is happening on the compositional surface of the text. The realist-oriented reader, intent on rationalizing a unitary persona as a plausible source for all this, is likely to overlook or look through the compositional dimension and conceptualize a poem that Chaucer never wrote. Chaucer's text consistently calls attention to itself as an assemblage and makes artful play of the relation in the narrative between the speaker and what is spoken. The evidence of the text, including the "blunders" that troubled Kittredge about the Pardoner's Tale and have troubled generations of realist interpreters of all of Chaucer's works, seems to require that we invert received interpretive opinion and recognize that drama, though by no means absent, is consistently subordinate to rhetoric, not vice versa. For Chaucer the artful rhetor, the text's speaker is a loosely defined instrumentality, not a realistically individualized source of expression or an end in itself.

Finally the Mánciple's Tale is comic in a serious epistemological sense. It is paradoxical that in this briefest of the Canterbury tales Chaucer explores more deeply than anywhere else in his works, possibly excepting the *House of Fame* and the ending of *Troilus,* the question that was never far from his consciousness. As an inquiry into the truth value of language, the Manciple's Tale is unusual because it discusses the problem so extensively and explicitly while at the same time displaying its implications in the compositional structure of the text. The conspicuous interplay of story and discourse emphasizes textuality. At the same time it destabilizes illusion as effectively as it creates it. Then in the story itself, as well as in the "digressive" discourse, questions about the validity and the efficacy of "telling" are prominently addressed. We might hope that marshaling both structural and thematic resources might finally produce an authoritative formulation of the philosophical status of language. But at the end Chaucer is as ambivalent as he was in the beginning, beguiled and skeptical both. The meaning of language is no more singular than the "moralite" of the Nun's Priest's Tale or any other tidings. We are told at the end to hold our tongue, to "be war, and be noon auctour newe / Of tidynges." The only answer is silence, but it is proclaimed in a torrent of language.

THE PARSON'S TALE

Fragment X, containing the Parson's Prologue and Tale and the Retraction, explicitly concludes the *Canterbury Tales* by proposing, in the Parson's words, "To knytte up al this feeste, and make an ende" (l. 47), and its opening lines link it with the preceding fragment:

> By that the Maunciple hadde his tale al ended,
> The sonne fro the south lyne was descended.

To the Host's impious request for a "fable . . . for cokkes
bones," the Parson responds with contempt for "fables and
swich wrecchednesse" (ll. 29–34). His message is truth. We
realize finally that Chaucer's destination, at the end of his literary journey through the contingencies of this world, is the
celestial Jerusalem, the truth that is not made by art or artifice
but simply *is*—or as close to it as his human language can
bring him. Fragment X is Chaucer's enactment of the one exception the Manciple's mother allowed in her exhortation to
silence at the close of the Manciple's Tale:

> "My sone, thy tonge sholdestow restreyne
> At alle tymes, but whan thou doost thy peyne
> To speke of God, in honour and preyere."
>
> (329–31)

A disappointment for many modern readers, and the first tale
to be jettisoned from school editions of the *Canterbury Tales*,
the Parson's Tale must nevertheless be regarded as a major
document in any assessment of Chaucer's poetics.

Chaucer's abandonment of narrative (and of verse) at the
end of the *Canterbury Tales* seems to signal a radical shift in his
orientation toward the question of authorship and the validity
of poetic truth. In the Parson's Tale Chaucer is indeed "noon
auctour newe / Of tidynges," as the Manciple's Tale finally ad-
monished, the Parson's Tale being a translation of two theological treatises, one on penitence and one on the seven deadly
sins. Yet its very size and its strategic placement as one of the
twin pillars, together with the General Prologue, that support
the structure of the *Tales* attest to its importance for Chaucer.
A poetic prayer, like the ending of *Troilus*, apparently would
not have fulfilled the need Chaucer felt for a massive *non*-
poetic, nonliterary conclusion to his literary pilgrimage.

Not only does the Parson's Tale abandon fiction and verse;
it also abandons the work's controlling illusion of a pilgrimage
to Canterbury. Although Fragment X is clearly Chaucer's conclusion for the *Canterbury Tales*, it does not reaffirm the narrative base established by "I" at the Tabard Inn. The closing

words are uttered not by the Chaucerian narrator but simply by the voice of the Parson's Tale concluding a treatise on penitence. The much-discussed frame of the tales is not in fact closed. Nor can we regard the Retraction (which we will consider shortly) as a closure of the Canterbury frame, since it establishes a different presentational level altogether. From an artistic and illusion-making point of view, it is clear that this great narrative of a pilgrimage ends in a digression.

Prevailing critical opinion is not congenial to such a perception. Rather than regard the Parson's Tale as a digression, it favors the view, as Ralph Baldwin puts it, that the Parson's Tale "musters into dramatic unity all the silent symmetries of the other tales and the *viage* as such." [10] In his evocation of the pilgrims individually wincing with guilt as the Parson expounds sins and excesses that Baldwin presumes they would respectively recognize as their own, Baldwin exemplifies an extreme form of creative interpretation and produces a "drama" where in fact we have only a treatise. Howard's view is more judicious but based on what seems to be a similar estimate of the unifying function of the Parson's Tale. For Howard the closing sentence of the Parson's Tale, with its cluster of spiritual paradoxes—glory purchased by lowness, plenty by hunger and thirst, life by death and the mortification of sin—"directs us to look back upon tales and groups of tales, to perform our own feat of memory." [11] I find no such direction in that concluding sentence, or indeed in the Parson's Tale as a whole, and such a discovery must be regarded as interpretive conjecture. The Parson's Tale is a devotional manual, or rather a combination of two such works. How it relates to the rest of the *Canterbury Tales* is an important question of poetics, and I think the answer depends on a clear understanding of the distinction I have tried to establish between interpretation and analysis. "The unity of the *Canterbury Tales*," as Baldwin entitled his influential monograph, refers only to an interpretive

10. Ralph Baldwin, *The Unity of the "Canterbury Tales," Anglistica* 5 (Copenhagen: Rosenkilde og Bagger, 1955), p. 99.
11. Howard, *The Idea of the Canterbury Tales*, p. 198.

construct. It is not a demonstrable feature of the text, available to objective analysis.

Before drawing out the implications of the Parson's Tale's disjunct relation with the body of the *Canterbury Tales*, I want to do justice to the spiritual interpretation that Baldwin articulated at a time when the roadside drama theory was generally applied in narrowly realistic and psychological terms. Pointing to the Parson's Prologue, Baldwin states (p. 96) that here is

> the time for recollection, the moment meant to qualify the pilgrims for their visit to Canterbury. . . . Here at last the metaphor is realized (it never hardens into allegory), because the Parson has expressly noted that he wishes to show them the way, "in this viage,"

> Of thilke parfit glorious pilgrimage
> That highte Jerusalem celestial.

The spiritual meaning of these lines (51–52) is unmistakable. Chaucer's use of the Christian metaphor effectively and movingly translates pilgrimage from earthly into heavenly terms. The transformation is sudden—coming without preparation after an attenuated earthly progress—and it is powerfully climactic. The Parson's Prologue also sounds a concluding note as the Host states that all tales but one have now been told and the Parson undertakes to "make an ende." As far as the frame goes, the Parson's Prologue *is* the end. But in attempting to fit the Parson's *Tale* into this frame Baldwin leaves analysis and turns to interpretive rationalization. The weakness of his monograph, as well as its value, as I pointed out elsewhere,[12] is that the "unity" it propounds is only frame deep. As for the vast body of the *Canterbury Tales*, including the Parson's Tale, Baldwin appropriates without qualification the roadside drama concept and dismisses the tales as "performances" that are "in a sense, the converse of the pilgrims themselves" (p. 78).

12. *Chaucer and the Shape of Creation* (Cambridge: Harvard Univ. Press, 1967), pp. 112–15.

As I have pointed out in these pages and elsewhere, the tales are too recalcitrant and rhetorically complex to be dismissed as mere characterizations of their speakers and instrumentalities in a supposedly larger psychological drama. The Parson's Tale is no exception to this caveat. It is no disservice to Chaucer's artistic integrity or to the artistry of the *Canterbury Tales* to recognize that the relation of the Parson's Tale to the frame is only momentary and superficial. It begins and ends with the Parson's Prologue. The tale that isn't a tale stands autonomously as a treatise of religious instruction, and its relation to its designated pilgrim teller is scarcely more than nominal. Having abandoned storytelling, Chaucer does not encounter in this treatise the presentational problem of making make-believe believable by way of a credible teller. Since Chaucer understands the truth told by the Parson's Tale to be not contingent but absolute, its voice is appropriately drained of human or dramatic content, at least to the extent that language can be depersonalized, as for example: "And now, sith I have declared yow what thyng is Penitence, now shul ye understonde that ther been three acciouns of Penitence" (l. 94). This voice bears no intrinsic relation to the pilgrim Parson. The disjunction bears out Howard's observation that the Parson's Tale "is not appropriate to the simple Parson of the General Prologue or the peremptory one who appears twice in the tales, and does not suit the situation in which he is supposed to speak it" (p. 175). Hearing this voice in our mind's ear, we might visualize—if we stretch our imagination—a monkish, selfless devotee of the Word of God, but hardly a country parson devoted to shepherding his flock. The tale does fulfill the intention of the angry Parson of the Parson's Prologue, who will heed St. Paul's reproof of "hem that weyven soothfastnesse / And tellen fables and swich wrecchednesse" (ll. 33–34). But it presents its "Moralitee and vertuous mateere" (l. 38) in a detached, nondramatized manner.

It seems, then, that in its ending the *Canterbury Tales* violates the integrity of its own structure, abandoning not only story and verse but also the Canterbury frame and its narrator. In attempting to assimilate this anomalous ending, critics have disregarded Genette's warning, which I think bears repeating in the present context: "It would be unfortunate, it seems to me, to seek 'unity' at any price, and in that way to *force* the work's coherence—which is of course one of criticism's strongest temptations . . . and also one most easy to satisfy, since all it requires is a little interpretive rhetoric."[13] Theories that either end with the Parson's Prologue or reside finally in the realm of tendentious "interpretive rhetoric" pay too high a price in forcing on the *Canterbury Tales* a unity it does not possess. As Genette says of Proust, we cannot deny in Chaucer the will for coherence and the striving for design, but equally undeniable in his work is the resistance of its matter, a resistance Chaucer chose to meet by accommodation rather than compromise. The difference is important because it determines whether constituent parts maintain their integrity or subordinate themselves to the whole.

The very irregularity of the Parson's Tale effects an ending perfectly consistent with the principles of Chaucer's poetics that we have educed in the course of this study. Chaucer wished to end the *Canterbury Tales* in piety, and the form of piety he chose was a homiletic manual of devotion. Rather than attempt to force this twofold treatise into conformity with the aesthetic design of a Canterbury pilgrimage, he chose to stretch the design to accommodate the treatise, regardless of the great bulge it produced. This indifference to symmetry and balance is consistent with what we have seen to be Chaucer's general mode of narrative composition, evident as early as the Ceyx and Alcione episode in the *Book of the Duchess*. Having established in the Parson's Prologue a figurative connection between earthly pilgrimage and heavenly salvation, Chaucer proceeded to elucidate the spiritual way. His method is amplification, an admired rhetorical device not only in its own right as adornment but, more important, as a means of *manifestatio*, or fullness of elucidation. As a digression that finally de-centers the *Canterbury*

---

13. Gérard Genette, *Narrative Discourse: An Essay in Method*, trans. Jane E. Lewin (Ithaca, N.Y.: Cornell Univ. Press, 1980), p. 266.

Tales, the Parson's Tale is analogous to the maternal discourse that brings the Manciple's Tale to a conclusion outside the narrative frame of its pilgrim teller. In a more general way, of course, self-sufficient digressions are commonplace in Chaucerian narrative.

The principle is further illustrated in the Parson's Tale itself in the long excursus on the seven deadly sins, which begins in the midst of part two (Confession) of the three-part exposition of penitence and goes on to overwhelm not only Confession but the entire treatise.[14] Characteristically, Chaucer does not scruple to "adjust" the deadly sins excursus so that it conforms stylistically to the treatise into which he inserts it. (Whether Chaucer placed it here or found it this way in his source is unknown and immaterial.) Though both texts observe conventions of theological discourse and Scriptural citation, many passages in the sins section rise to an emotional fervor alien to the relentlessly orderly expository voice of the treatise on penitence. For example, there is nothing in the treatise on penitence stylistically comparable to this description of Anger:

> For certes, outrageous wratthe dooth al that evere the devel hym comaundeth; for he ne spareth neither Crist ne his sweete Mooder. / And in his outrageous anger and ire, allas! allas! ful many oon at that tyme feeleth in his herte ful wikkedly, both of Crist and eek of alle his halwes. / Is nat this a cursed vice? Yis, certes.
>
> (557–59)

As in so many other instances, Chaucer in the Parson's Tale is more concerned to present individuated materials in their fullness and integrity than to compromise for the sake of presentational consistency and structural cohesiveness.

As I have suggested, the Parson's Tale is Chaucer's second ending, the ending of the *Canterbury Tales.* It follows the end of fictions, the Manciple's Tale, and precedes Chaucer's valediction to his poetic career, the Retraction. It completes a

---

14. For a detailed rhetorical analysis of the Parson's Tale see my *Chaucer and the Shape,* chap. 11.

work whose greatness is universally acknowledged and whose freshness and staying power transcend generations of critics whose diverse and often conflicting presuppositions and expectations are all somehow satisfied in this great evocation of God's plenty. In the view of the *Canterbury Tales* proposed here we have flattened out the text, as it were, and tried to trace the maker's hand as it reveals itself not only in the making of fictions but in the making of makers of fictions. When we readjust our perceptions in accordance with Chaucer's rhetorical orientation to poetic makings, we find that Chaucer generally subordinates verisimilitude to compositional considerations. It is not that Chaucer is uninterested or unskilled in persuasive and "dramatic" representation—far from it—but that he incorporates the illusion of reality into the larger dimension of a conscious literary artistry. For Chaucer realistic illusion is artifice, and the language that produces it is real. His art reaches beyond realism to contemplate language itself and to record a sensitive and skilled poet's lifelong engagement with that problematic medium.

As did earlier generations, readers today discover in Chaucer something fundamentally attuned to their own perceptions of art, language, and the world. As I have tried to show, the *Canterbury Tales*, like the dream visions, is "postmodern" in its manifest awareness of the contingent and arbitrary nature of language. The structures of language—such as the illusion of a medieval pilgrimage or a postmodern plot—are from moment to moment subject to interruption, redefinition, transformation. Structural stability, like the things of this world, is not to be trusted for long. Meaning, refracted through multiple styles of discourse and angles of perception, is not fixed and singular but is inevitably contingent on the language that purports to capture it. Perhaps Chaucer's most striking affirmation of the contingency of meaning is found in the Clerk's Tale and the envoi that stands that noble tale on its head. But there is ample evidence throughout his works, as we have noted particularly in the *House of Fame* and the Nun's Priest's Tale, that Chaucer was poignantly aware that although moralities may be derived, they too are words, more "tidings," enlightening in their way and in their time but not in all ways and for all time. What does remain is language itself, reflecting its author's ambivalent consciousness of its powers and its limitations.

For a rhetorical poet like Chaucer, meaning dances elusively among the interstices of discourse and the spaces between his own mind, the text he is composing, and the illusion his text creates. The heterogeneity of the *Canterbury Tales* cannot be persuasively interpreted away or subsumed by a theory of unity, for the *Tales* expresses Chaucer's fascination with multiplicity, his lifelong devotion to—or continuing experimentation with—the diverse modes of human discourse. Against the design of the *Tales* Chaucer's materials exert continuing pressures of their own, and similarly within individual tales conceptual unity often gives way to digressive bursts, and internal cohesion often defers to shapely fragments.

THE RETRACTION

In his last ending Chaucer takes leave of his lifelong dedication to writing. That the Retraction is a personal statement by the author of the *Canterbury Tales* and of the numerous other works named in this recantation is not universally acknowledged by Chaucerians. Two issues are in contention. The first concerns interpretation of the phrase "this litel tretys" in the first sentence of the Retraction: "Now preye I hem alle that herkne this litel tretys or rede, that if ther be any thyng in it that liketh hem. . . ." Does the phrase refer to the just-completed Parson's Tale or to the *Canterbury Tales* as a whole? If the former, the speaker would presumably be the Parson, not Chaucer, and the Retraction would be at least in part a dramatic projection rather than a personal statement. The second issue is the sincerity of the Retraction and Fragment X as a whole, some scholars arguing for an ironic reading, which would see Fragment X, including the Retraction, as another rhetorical set piece in the Canterbury array.

There is something to be said for both sides of both of these issues, though on the issue of irony the weight of critical opinion seems to acknowledge the penitential earnestness of the ending.[15] On the question of whose ending the Retraction is, the Parson's or Chaucer's, the contention is more complex. Douglas Wurtele has made a just assessment of the opposing views and has offered a shrewd proposal for reconciliation.[16] As he demonstrates, logic and semantics support the view of Donaldson, Robinson, and others that the Retraction's first sentence attaches it to the Parson's Tale. Yet the fifth sentence (l. 1085) of the Retraction introduces an authorial frame of reference and a personal tone that cannot be attributed to the Parson. I quote from the fourth sentence to illustrate the break at "and namely":

> Wherfore I biseke yow mekely, for the mercy of God, that ye preye for me that Crist have mercy on me and foryeve me my giltes; / and namely of my translacions and enditynges of worldly vanitees, the whiche I revoke in my retracciouns: / as is the book of Troilus; the book also of Fame; the book of the xxv. Ladies; the book of the Duchesse; the book of Seint Valentynes day of the Parlement of Briddes; the tales of Caunterbury, thilke that sownen into synne.

Wurtele recognizes a certain "awkwardness" here, as the Retraction abruptly veers away from general and arguably conventional piety into a personal recantation and prayer, only to return, at line 1090[b], to a language and tone more appropriate to the Parson. Wurtele concludes that the citation of specific works and the prayer for personal grace (ll. 1085–90[a]) are an interpolation embedded in the Parson's last words. Such a reading, recognizing an inconsistency in the presentational voice, is by no means inconsistent with Chaucer's practice as we have perceived it throughout his works. In fact it is

15. See Rodney Delasanta, "Penance and Poetry in the *Canterbury Tales*," *PMLA* 93 (1978): 240–47, which reaffirms the "orthodox" view of Robinson, Donaldson, Baldwin, Robertson, and others and effectively responds to "ironists" such as Sayce, Finlayson, and Allen.

16. Douglas Wurtele, "The Penitence of Geoffrey Chaucer," *Viator* 11 (1980): 335–59.

altogether fitting that Chaucer's valediction should be composed in the mode of rhetorical collage and that the identity of its voice(s) should be problematic.

What is unique about at least part of the Retraction is the glimpse it affords us of the poet's own unmediated, undramatized sense of his human position. He looks to his past and his future, his writings and his salvation. His vision upward toward God, though not free of anxiety, expresses confidence in an absolute that endures beyond the contingencies of this world. His vision downward, surveying his worldly makings, is less confident and more ambivalent; it certifies some works and recants others.

Chaucer's poetics is a program of this world, and as such it accommodates all the uncertainties and indeterminacies of worldly experience, including trust and distrust of literary authorities. It is a wonderfully flexible and expansive poetics, fundamentally heterodox, open to all modes of discourse, and indifferent to strictures of orthodoxy, whether moral, philosophical, aesthetic, or generic. It is this insubordinate attitude that brings Chaucer's poetics into such sympathetic resonance with postmodernism. Chaucerian and postmodern poetics share a capacity to accommodate extraordinarily diverse materials and to do so without sacrificing the integrity of these components. Thus, for example, the *Canterbury Tales* finds a place for didactic prose among poetic fictions, for pious tales as well as ribald ones, for both realism and stylization, for truth and countertruth. Similarly inclusive in its heterodoxy, a work such as Vladimir Nabokov's *Pale Fire* is both poetry and prose, narrative and document, a beguiling mixture of imaginary quest and real (though really parodic) scholarship. Chaucer's frequent verbal extravagances—his stylistic parodies and encyclopedic inventories, for example—often indulged in for their own sake, regardless of imperatives of generic or stylistic cohesion, have something in common with postmodernist writers' stylistic virtuosity and heterogeneousness, exemplified in Joyce's verbal displays in *Ulysses*, or Gilbert Sorrentino's five-page inventory of imaginary titles in *Mulligan Stew*. The common ground is a perceptible and often prominent self-reflexiveness that can be as profound and troubled for Chaucer as for Beckett and Barth and many another "experimental" writer. Or it can give rise to artful play—play with art and its illusions as well as play with words—that may be parodic, ironic, or ambiguously indeterminate—or simply exuberant.

But if the critical theory and "experimental" practice of our own time help us to define Chaucer's poetics, we must also recognize the limits of the comparison. In the final analysis Chaucer's position is not postmodern but premodern. It is not fully medieval in the Augustinian sense, yet the Parson's Tale and the Retraction, like the ending of *Troilus,* are clear signs that Chaucer's poetics is not completely adrift from the universal frame of Christian theology. When Chaucer turned to thoughts of a final reckoning, he could place himself in a God-centered, universal order, within which resolution of this world's uncertainties was still attainable. Chaucer's Retraction—at least part of it—is a statement of faith in an uncircumscribable absolute that circumscribes all that is contingent and problematic in this world, including tidings and their bearers. Since this faith does not permeate and shape the *Canterbury Tales,* as it does Dante's *Commedia,* for example, we are perhaps justified in questioning the sincerity of Chaucer's orthodoxy. But that is a question we can never answer. What we can say, on the evidence of his works, is that Chaucer could participate in two epistemologies. As a Christian he could locate himself, through the fixed truths of God's language and Christian prayer, in a stable universal reality. As a poet, making the world for himself with the arbitrary and conventional language of man, he could not command that divine reality. His human fixities were momentary and contingent, and his human position was uncertain.

Chaucer was as ambivalent as the postmodern writer about the efficacy of his language and about his own position as an arbiter between truth and falsehood or between truth and countertruth. But if he was uncertain about his position in the temporal, historical world, he could still place himself, alternatively, in a stable, supranatural reality whose language was unambiguously true. He could "Unto the world leve now to be thral," as he urged in the ballade "Truth," and through prayer to the God of all he could attain the deliverance of truth. Even though that reality was undergoing dissolution in Chaucer's time and its persuasive power was waning, it nevertheless provided a comprehensive and unified system in which language and reality interpenetrated in a fixed embodiment of truth. Postmodernism offers no such vision beyond itself of an absolute and of absolution. Like Chaucer, the postmodern writer is ambivalent about his position in this world, but unlike Chaucer he has no supraterrestrial refuge. He is "lost in the cosmos," as Walker Percy entitled his book describing the contemporary situation.[17] Chaucer too, as a wayfarer in the language of this world, was not always sure where he was, though when he looked beyond language he knew where he wanted to go.

17. Walker Percy, *Lost in the Cosmos: The Last Self-Help Book* (New York: Washington Square Press), 1983.

Index